WHY THE
SENATE SLEPT

WHY THE SENATE SLEPT

The Gulf of Tonkin Resolution
and the Beginning of
America's Vietnam War

EZRA Y. SIFF

Foreword by
Lt. Col. Anthony B. Herbert
U.S. Army, Retired

PRAEGER

Westport, Connecticut
London

Library of Congress Cataloging-in-Publication Data

Siff, Ezra Y., 1942–
    Why the senate slept : the Gulf of Tonkin resolution and the
    beginning of America's Vietnam war / Ezra Y. Siff ; foreword by Lt.
    Col. Anthony B. Herbert.
        p.   cm.
    Includes bibliographical references (p.   ) and index.
    ISBN 0–275–96389–6 (alk. paper)
    1. Tonkin Gulf Incidents, 1964.   2. Vietnamese Conflict,
    1961–1975—United States.   I. Title.
    DS557.8.T6S54   1999
    959.704'3—dc21   98–25612

British Library Cataloguing in Publication Data is available.

Library of Congress Catalog Card Number: 98–25612
ISBN: 0–275–96389–6

First published in 1999

Praeger Publishers, 88 Post Road West, Westport, CT 06881
An imprint of Greenwood Publishing Group, Inc.

Printed in the United States of America

∞

The paper used in this book complies with the
Permanent Paper Standard issued by the National
Information Standards Organization (Z39.48–1984).

10 9 8 7 6 5 4 3 2 1

Copyright Acknowledgments

The author and the publisher gratefully acknowledge permission for use of the following
material:

Permission to reprint Gaylord Nelson's October 2, 1964 letter to the *New York Times* is
granted by Senator Nelson.

Excerpts from the interview conducted by Ezra Siff on May 2, 1996 with Senator Gaylord
Nelson is used by permission from interviewee.

Dedicated in memory of Senator Wayne Morse,
a giant of the United States Senate.

"And say not thou 'My country right or wrong'
Nor shed thy blood for an unhallowed cause."

—John Quincy Adams, in CONGRESS, *Slavery and an Unjust War.*

CONTENTS

A photo essay follows page 59

FOREWORD

"Vietnam" was a tragedy, for Vietnam and for the United States. No further explanation need be required on that point.

The blame for this tragedy has been sprayed about the scenery much like machine-gun-fire in the hands of a recruit. It was the "press" and "television"; or the "politicians," Eisenhower, Kennedy, or Johnson; the "professional officers' corps"; the "Hippies"; the "draft"; the "youth who couldn't measure up."

While the truth is even though some of these, namely some isolated generals—Harkins, Westmoreland and Abrams—along with some of the lower ranks of the ilk who gave us My Lai—Koster, Henderson, Medina and Calley—combined with presidential incompetence, were in great part responsible for our loss in Vietnam, they in no way were responsible for its creation. That distinction, Ezra Siff singles out as direct and true as an expert's long thrust of the bayonet, belongs to no one other than Robert McNamara and McGeorge Bundy. And it is owned by them as World War II belongs to Germany and Japan.

J. William Fulbright, Chairman of the prestigious Foreign Relations Committee, and Richard B. Russell, Chairman of the powerful Armed Forces Committee, played their roles by their noted absences of personal integrity and courage. As did some other more minor players (Where were the future doves?), who fell into line behind Johnson. But despite the spin, it was not LBJ's War. It was McNamara's and Bundy's. And it is on both their heads, above all others, that the blame for so many hundreds of thousands of deaths must be heaped.

McNamara now says he's sorry. He tries to excuse it as policy that spun out of control, beyond his power to influence, never seeming to realize, as Siff has so clearly demonstrated, that there was no "policy." There was only daily so-called "best and brightest" reactions that were no better than a battered prize-fighter to each and every fluctuation in seriatim. It was their own ignorance in foreign affairs that kept "tightening the screw a bit more," even when they knew it would no longer work, as we now know from McNamara's own recent confession!

This contention by Ezra Siff would also be unbelievable if the evidence presented were not so overwhelming. The undeniable truths are presented and the blame is clearly established. No understanding of what has become "Vietnam" can be complete without this book, the only book I know that lays the cause of that war directly where it belongs—in the House and Senate of the United States of America, both of which "slept" while Bundy and McNamara created their nightmare.

Lt. Col. Anthony B. Herbert*

*Most decorated battalion commander of the Vietnam War.

ACKNOWLEDGMENTS

I wish to express my deepest gratitude to those without whose assistance this book would never have been.

To the first to provide the idea for the book's scope and direction, Dr. Gar Alperovitz of Washington. Gar was Senator Nelson's legislative director in August 1964 and immediately recognized the significance of the seemingly innocuous Gulf of Tonkin Resolution.

To Professor Lloyd Gardner of Rutgers University for his constant advice and support.

To Harvey Morrell, without whose librarian skills I would have been lost. Harvey found every book, article, and Congressional Record microfilm that was needed, and with unfailing speed, cheerfulness, and grace.

To Mrs. Dawn Evans and Mrs. Barbara Jones for deciphering my hideous scrawl and producing the computer disk. In a different time and a different place, they would have been assigned to serve at Bletchley Park.

To my dear friend Bill Spring of Boston, for his constant encouragement. How many are left who remember Hugh Casey's joint?

To Senators Nelson and McGovern for their generosity in spending time with me and sharing their memories in the interviews. During the 1960s, as the war escalated and ultimately led to involvement of 500,000 American ground troops, I was a legislative assistant to Senator Nelson. I served with him from late 1965 to 1968.

To Miss Joan Mutz, a former Nelson staff member, who met me in

Madison, Wisconsin, to go through Senator Nelson's files at the Historical Society there. Joan alone knew what was in each box, since they had not yet been catalogued.

To Chris McNally, former student, current friend.

And to Ms. Linda Ellis, the production editor at Greenwood Publishing Group, whose kind advice and encouragement were of tremendous help.

If I have overlooked anyone, please forgive the oversight.

PROLOGUE

"This resolution will pass and Senators who vote for it will live to regret it."

—Senator Wayne Morse (D.-Oreg.)[1]

At the beginning of America's wars, a building tension and sense of crisis had always existed before hostilities began. Secession led to the ultimate outbreak of the Civil War. World War I had begun in 1914, and America became a combatant in 1917. Pressures through the late 1930s, culminating with the failed negotiations with Japan in November 1941, led to Pearl Harbor. In Korea, there was a clear invasion of the South. No such expectancy ever centered on Vietnam in August 1964.

Although in the preceding several years a small number of U.S. military advisors had suffered some casualties, no threat of major conflict was felt.

This critical factor contributed heavily to the shock of President Lyndon B. Johnson's choice to deliver a dramatic message on radio and television at 11:36 P.M. on August 4, 1964. President Johnson was severely criticized for his timing of the announcement, which preceded the actual air strike. Congressman Edgar Foreman (R.-Tex.) said, "We have heard a lot about trigger-happy irresponsibility lately . . . about Goldwater. . . . But what kind of responsibility is this where the President goes on radio and TV and tells them, the communists, one and a half hours in advance, that the air strike is coming?"[2] The substance of the events and reaction to them fell short of the drama inherent in their announcement.

President Johnson said:

> My fellow Americans:
>
> As President and Commander in Chief, it is my duty to the American people to report that renewed hostile actions against United States' ships on the high seas in the Gulf of Tonkin have today required me to order the military forces of the United States to take action in reply.
>
> The initial attack on the destroyer Maddox on August 2nd was repeated today by a number of hostile vessels attacking two U.S. destroyers with torpedoes. The destroyers and supporting aircraft acted at once on the orders I gave after initial act of aggression. We believe at least two of the attacking boats were sunk. There were no U.S. losses.[3]

According to the President, the U.S. Navy had been attacked on the high seas. The President announced that he would "immediately request the Congress to pass a resolution making it clear that our government is united . . . to take all necessary measures in support of freedom in Southeast Asia."[4]

Yet a nagging sense of skepticism lingered. The attacks, assuming they occurred, were at most isolated incidents. There was no massive coordinated attack on the U.S. fleet such as at Pearl Harbor. No invasion force was moving over the borders of a U.S. ally such as in Korea. Nevertheless, Johnson chose to inflate the incidental, almost non-event, into a major crisis that required immediate passage of a warlike congressional resolution. Some believe Lyndon Johnson's long expertise as Majority Leader of the Senate caused him to want a resolution of support from Congress even before he himself knew what his long-term response would be, to ensure that he was covered by full congressional support.

The day before LBJ's dramatic midnight speech on August 3 in response to what the administration termed the attack upon the destroyer *Maddox*, LBJ issued the following order:

> I have instructed the Navy (1) to continue the patrols in the Gulf of Tonkin off the coast of North Vietnam, (2) to double the force by adding an additional destroyer to the one already on patrol, (3) to provide a combat air patrol over the destroyers, and (4) to issue orders to the commanders of the combat aircraft and the

two destroyers (a) to attack any force which attacks them in international waters, and (b) to attack with the objective not only of driving off the force, but of destroying it.[5]

President Johnson's resolution was sent to the Congress the next morning, August 5. The joint House and Senate resolution numbered S.J. 189 contained a provision that proved through the following bitter years to be extremely controversial. Section 2 included language "[that] . . . the United States is therefore prepared as the President determines to take all necessary steps, including the use of armed forces to assist [South Vietnam]."[6]

The resolution was immediately attacked by Senator Morse, whose main constitutional argument throughout his long and isolated opposition to administration policy was, as he stated that day, "Article I, Section 8 of our Constitution does not permit the President to make war at his discretion,"[7] an argument previously made by Senator Robert Taft (R.-Ohio) when President Harry Truman committed U.S. forces to enter into combat in Korea in 1950.[8]

Morse beseeched J. W. Fulbright (D.-Ark.) to hold legitimate hearings, since there was no impending emergency. We had not been attacked on a massive scale such as followed Pearl Harbor. He warned Fulbright that the language was too broad. Morse wished to hear testimony of "dovish generals" such as Matthew Ridgway, James Gavin, David Shoup, and Joseph Collins.[9] Ridgway was a World War II hero who later succeeded General Douglas MacArthur as Commander of UN forces in Korea. Gavin was the youngest general officer of World War II and parachuted with his troops during the predawn hours at Normandy. General Shoup was the former Commandant of the Marine Corps.

Fulbright insisted that a state of emergency existed and that the legislative process be accelerated. So, instead of deliberative hearings which would have set all aspects of Vietnam's war before the Senate and the public, the old LBJ style utilized in pushing through domestic legislation was again used—accelerated hearings, minimum number of witnesses, limited debate, unanimous consent agreements.

Equally at fault was Senator Mike Mansfield (D.-Mont.), Senate Majority Leader and later a leading dove. It is the majority leader who sets the Senate agenda and leads the orchestration of debate time. So even if Fulbright as Chairman of the Foreign Relations Committee could, on his own, limit the hearings, it was Mansfield who was responsible for permitting the limited floor debate and unanimous consent voting agreements. These came at the discretion of the majority leadership.

These rush tactics succeeded in achieving rapid passage of S.J. 189. Hearings on the resolution were held August 6 by the Senate Foreign

Relations and Armed Services Committees sitting together with the House Foreign Affairs and Military Affairs Committees. Three witnesses testified, Secretary of State Dean Rusk, Secretary of Defense Robert McNamara, and the Chairman of the Joint Chiefs of Staff, General Earle Wheeler. The hearings were adjourned after one hour and forty minutes.[10] The text of the hearings was not published until late in 1966, more than two years later. The printed hearings were heavily censored, making them of little use to a researcher even today.[11] The resolution passed with only Senator Morse, a member of the Senate Foreign Relations Committee, voting "no."

As Chairman of the Foreign Relations Committee, Senator Fulbright became floor manager of S.J. 189; his job was to defend the resolution and guide it toward passage. During Johnson's Senate days, he and Fulbright were considered national Democrats despite being southerners. Johnson would refer to Fulbright as his "Secretary of State," when they were both senators, Fulbright having great expertise in foreign affairs and Johnson having none.

Using the old Johnson tactics, Majority Leader Mansfield obtained a unanimous consent agreement to limit debate to three hours—three hours on an issue with which most senators were not even remotely familiar. The vote would come the next day, requiring senators to acquaint themselves literally overnight with the question of whether we were really at war or some version short of war, and over what issue. Were the attacks on the ships an isolated incident or the beginning of a war? If the latter, the North Vietnamese seem to have chosen a rather inauspicious manner in which to attack the United States.

There were presumptions taken as fact, as when Senator Richard B. Russell stated, "certainly no foreign nation has a right to challenge our use of the high seas. We have a right to be there."[12] He presumed the position of the administration to be true—that our ships were on the high seas on routine patrol.

Besides Senator Morse, other senators had reservations. Senator George McGovern (D.-S.D.) raised the obvious question, "All of us have been puzzled, if not baffled as to why a little state such as North Vietnam should seek a deliberate naval conflict with the United States with the overwhelming naval and air power that we have in that area."[13]

But none of the senators appeared to question the actual facts as presented by the administration. The only senator who attempted to delineate the exact meaning of the vaguely worded section 2 of the resolution was Senator Gaylord Nelson (D.-Wis.). Despite the great rush to get the resolution through, Senator Nelson, on August 7, minutes before the three-hour limit for debate ran out, offered an amendment to section 2 to clarify and create a history of legislative intent of the meaning of the resolution. The amendment read:

(b) The Congress also approves and supports the effort of the President to bring the problem of peace in Southeast Asia to the Security Council of the United Nations, and the President's declaration that the United States, seeking no extension of the present military conflict, will respond to provocation in a manner that is "limited and fitting." Our continuing policy is to limit our role to the provision of aid, training assistance, and military advice, and it is the sense of Congress that except when provoked to a greater response, we should continue to attempt to avoid a direct military involvement in the Southeast Asian conflict.[14]

Fulbright answered that the Nelson amendment is what S.J. 189 itself meant. He refused to accept the amendment since that would require sending it back to the House, necessitating a conference committee, and precious time would be lost.

Final passage of S.J. 189 in the House was 414–0 and in the Senate 88–2, Senators Morse and Gruening voting "no." President Johnson signed it the same day, August 7. Nelson's "aye" vote at the time was based on Fulbright's assurances. This would not occur again.

Thus was precipitated not only the human tragedy of the eight-year Vietnam War, but a major constitutional crisis as the legislative branch failed to temper the unilateral use of executive power in conducting a war without effective Congressional oversight and contrary to the Congress' constitutional duty.

This book focuses on the lack of response by the U.S. Senate during those early days of the Vietnam war when forceful action by the Congress could have changed the policy which was really being carried out by the President and a very few others without restraint. Special focus will be upon Senators Fulbright and Russell—Fulbright for his inconsistencies, and Russell for his consistent opposition and inexplicable silence.

Intensified hostilities, rising casualties, and increased bombing caused James Reston to write in the *New York Times* on February 14, 1965: "This country is in an undeclared and unexplained war in Vietnam. . . . But the fact is that we are in a war that is not only undeclared and unexplained, but that has not even been widely debated in the Congress or the country."

It is my goal to attempt to explain why the issue was not "widely debated in the Congress" and why the U.S. Senate failed to exercise its constitutional duty.

NOTES

1. Cong. Rec. S18425 (Daily ed., Aug. 6, 1964).
2. Michael Beschloss, *Taking Charge: The Johnson White Houses Tapes, 1963–64*

(New York: Simon and Schuster, 1997), p. 507 n. 5. President Johnson's reaction to Foreman's remarks were not benevolent. In August he told Speaker John Mc-Cormack, "I just wanted to point out this little shit-ass Foreman today got up and said that we acted impulsively." Ibid., p. 508.

3. *Public Papers of the President, Lyndon B. Johnson* #498, 1964. The full text of the President's speech is in Appendix I.

4. Ibid.

5. *Public Papers, Lyndon B. Johnson* #197. This was read to reporters by the President, and he took no questions. Eugene Windchy, *Tonkin Gulf* (Garden City, N.Y.: Doubleday, 1971), p. 5.

6. The entire text of S.J. 189 is in Cong. Rec. S18133 (Daily ed., Aug. 5, 1964). See Appendix II.

7. Cong. Rec. S18133 (Daily ed., Aug. 5, 1964).

8. It must be recognized that there are obvious distinctions between Truman's actions in June 1950 and Johnson's Gulf of Tonkin Resolution. Truman had already committed U.S. forces in the face of a raging war being carried out by the North Korean invasion. Johnson was not dealing with an invasion and later tried to use the resolution as a congressional endorsement of his action. Truman never went to Congress for any resolution of support.

Nevertheless, Senator Taft's remarks are of interest in their similarity to the future Vietnam dissent.

Mr. Taft. Mr. President, I have only a few words to say on the legal right of the President's act.

Although I should be willing to vote to approve the President's new policy as a policy, and give support to our forces in Korea, I think it is proper and essential that we discuss at this time the right and power of the President to do what he has done. I hope others will discuss it, because I have not thoroughly investigated the question of the right and the power of the President to do what he has done.

His action unquestionably has brought about a de facto war with the Government of northern Korea. He has brought that war about without consulting Congress and without congressional approval. We have a situation in which a far distant part of the world one nation has attacked another, and if the President can intervene in Korea without congressional approval, he can go to war in Malaya or Indonesia or Iran. . . .

Mr. President, Korea itself is not vitally important to the United States. It is hard to defend. We have another instance of communism picking out a soft spot where the Communists feel that they can make a substantial advance and can obtain a moral victory without risking war. From the past philosophy and declarations of our leaders, it was not unreasonable for the North Koreans to suppose that they could get away with it and that we would do nothing about it. Cong. Rec. S9320–1 (Daily ed., June 28, 1950).

9. David Halberstam, *The Best and the Brightest* (New York: Random House, 1969), p. 417.

10. See Southeast Asia Resolution, p. 3 and p. 15. The complete text of the resolution is contained in Appendix II.

11. Ernest Gruening and Herbert W. Beaser, *Vietnam Folly* (Washington, D.C.: National Press, 1968), p. 242.

12. Cong. Rec. S18403 (Daily ed., Aug. 6, 1964).

13. Ibid., S18402.

14. Ibid., S18459. A key impetus in creation of the amendment was Dr. Gar

Alperovitz, then legislative director of Senator Nelson's staff. Today, Dr. Alperovitz is a world-renowned historian. In a 1996 interview, Alperovitz told the author that he didn't believe a word of the administration's version of the facts. Later in this book we shall see that his skepticism was justified.

INTRODUCTION

Most Americans familiar with the history of the Vietnam war regard it as President Lyndon Johnson's war. They also believe that critical policy decisions were made by a very small group of so-called "hawkish advisors"—Secretary of Defense Robert McNamara, Secretary of State Dean Rusk, and National Security advisors McGeorge Bundy and Walt Rostow. Those with a deeper understanding recognize that Johnson did not want to be pushed into either an air war or a ground war. He feared another Korean-type stalemate, which would destroy his dreams of a Great Society.

A propaganda myth, put forth by the military with great success, was that the reason we did not win in Vietnam was that our forces were restrained from using their full war-making capabilities. Had the Air Force been permitted to bomb Hanoi and mine Hiaphong Harbor, without allowing the enemy sanctuaries, the result would have been "victory." This theory adroitly ignores the likelihood that such use of full power would have brought either Soviet or Chinese intervention, and as Senator George Aiken (R.-Vt.),[1] a long-time friend and confidant of President Johnson, said, the world would stand at the edge of total destruction. LBJ himself, in March 1964, quoted press anxiety "that psychologically we're approaching the Yalu River again, where Chinese, and possibly Russian, intervention must be expected."[2]

While it is true that the war was initiated by President Johnson and that policy was set by a small group of advisors, the thesis of this book is that they do not bear the entire responsibility for the most disastrous foreign policy tragedy in U.S. history. That responsibility was shared heavily by the Congress of the United States, and by the Senate in particular. At the time of passage of the Gulf of Tonkin Resolution, few senators were fully aware of what was occurring in Vietnam. Even in the very beginning, however, there were some senators who were deeply involved in the Vietnamese question and were bitterly opposed to any form of American intervention in what they regarded as an indigenous civil war.

The administration drew its greatest support during those crucial early months from Senator Richard Russell (D.-Ga.),[3] Chairman of the Armed Services Committee, long considered to be the Senate's foremost authority on military matters; and from Senator J. William Fulbright (D.-Ark.), Chairman of the Senate Committee on Foreign Relations.

Fulbright was graduated as a Rhodes scholar from Oxford, England, in 1928, and, as an attorney, from George Washington University in 1934. He served in the House during World War II and was elected to the U.S. Senate in 1944, serving until his defeat in the 1974 primary. President Kennedy had seriously considered nominating him for the office of Secretary of State, but his segregationist record eliminated him.[4]

At least one scholar has written that, in 1964, Fulbright was "not particularly knowledgeable about Vietnam."[5]

Both Russell and Fulbright were long-time friends of LBJ, Russell having become Johnson's mentor when LBJ first won his Senate seat in 1948. It was through the influence of Russell that the first-term Senator Johnson became Democratic leader in the Senate, an unheard-of departure from a protocol which dictated selection for leadership positions through seniority.

Russell and Fulbright were the primary Senate advocates of administration policy during those early months following the Tonkin Resolution, although their support was based upon different reasons. Russell was bitterly opposed to any U.S. military involvement in Vietnam and had been since before the French defeat there in 1954—almost as vehemently as was Senator Wayne Morse (D.-Oreg.).[6] His position from the very beginning was that U.S. military intervention could not succeed. Nevertheless, he refused to publicly oppose Johnson, despite his constant private warnings to him.

Even McNamara began to have second thoughts about the administration's policy toward the end of 1966.[7] Indeed, McNamara moved through the levels of Johnson's esteem from "The ablest man I've ever met," upon the President's taking office,[8] to "You've never seen such a lot of shit" in response to a McNamara memo of mid-1967.[9]

Yet, despite this opposition from the Chairman of the Armed Services

Committee from the outset, and the growing doubts of Secretary McNamara, prime architect of the Johnson administration policy, neither man was sufficiently courageous to speak out publicly.

Senator Fulbright's support for the administration position was crucial during those early months. Fulbright was the floor manager for the Gulf of Tonkin Resolution. As a foremost authority on foreign policy, senators with little or no background on the Vietnam question were inclined to follow and be comforted by his lead. Although years later Fulbright conceded that his role was the greatest mistake of his career, his prestige and, at the time, his influence carried Johnson's resolution. He failed, after all the years of having dealt with Lyndon Johnson, to realize the reality of what was occurring. Indeed, not fully grasping the import of what he was involved in, he referred to the resolution in a private conversation with Senator Gaylord Nelson (D.-Wis.) as a meaningless "cheerleader" resolution.[10]

Although Fulbright was an acknowledged factor at the outset, a cursory examination of his position on other matters reveals, despite his subsequent canonization, this flawed sense of judgment.

After Fulbright became the Fulbright of Lamentations, abandoning his previous role of one of the prime false prophets, he was quoted by historian Doris Kearns Goodwin as saying, "Roosevelt's deviousness in a good cause made it easier for Lyndon Johnson to practice the same kind of deviousness in a bad cause,"[11] which reveals a misstated interpretation of the facts. Roosevelt's pro-British and anti-Nazi position was known and had been debated in public and in Congress for years prior to World War II. Didn't Senator Fulbright remember America First, headed by Lindbergh, whom FDR believed to be a Nazi? Did he not recall the debate in Congress over H.R. 1776 which, by only one vote, extended the draft in 1941? Wasn't he aware of people such as Senator Burton Wheeler (D.-Mont.) who attacked FDR and his policies for years? It was only after the resolution was passed that LBJ's deviousness began to run the Vietnam War.

During the Cuban missile crisis, Fulbright opposed the adoption of the blockade, thought to be too weak a position, and favored military action.[12] President Kennedy was confounded by the inconsistencies in Fulbright's position. In 1961, Fulbright argued against the Bay of Pigs invasion saying, "The Castro regime is a thorn in the flesh, but it is not a dagger in the heart." But in the 1962 crisis he favored an invasion.[13] Today, many still believe that military action, bombing, or an invasion would have caused a Soviet nuclear response,[14] and that President Kennedy had the wisdom to avoid that risk.

There was from the beginning a small group of senators skeptical of the Johnson administration's policy and future goals. The primary opponent was Senator Wayne Morse (D.-Oreg.).[15] Senator Morse held a seat on the Foreign Relations Committee and was a long-time expert, especially in matters of the Far East. Interestingly, on July 27, 1945, immediately after the Senate voted its approval of the United Nations Charter, Senator Morse delivered a detailed, almost prophetic, speech concerning the need for the United States to act swiftly to counter Soviet interference in Korea. Korea was a country few Americans had heard of. In fact, the United States really had no postwar policy planned.[16] Failure of the State Department to follow Morse's advice to immediately support a provisional Korean government to replace the beaten Japanese caused both Korea and this country to pay a heavy, bitter price in the resulting so-called "Korean Police Action."

Another important and unexpected development in the Gulf of Tonkin Resolution debate was the emergence of Senator Gaylord Nelson (D.-Wis.) as a leader of the opposition to administration policy. Gaylord Nelson was born in Clear Lake, Wisconsin. He was graduated from the University of Wisconsin Law School in 1942 and then served four years as a lieutenant in the U.S. Army; he fought in the brutal battle for Okinawa in the spring of 1945. After the war, he was elected to the Wisconsin state legislature, serving as Democratic leader of the state senate for eight years. Following two terms as governor, in 1962 he was elected to the U.S. Senate. Thus, in the summer of 1964 he was a freshman senator from the midwest with no particular background in foreign affairs. Nelson first spoke out publicly against U.S. involvement in the war in Vietnam in November 1962, while still governor of Wisconsin, as well as after his election to the Senate. In an interview on a Wisconsin television station, he said involvement in the Vietnamese civil war would be a terrible mistake.[17]

It was both unusual and dramatic for a first-term senator with no previous expertise in foreign affairs to confront and challenge the Chairman of the Foreign Relations Committee. Nelson knew he couldn't win, but he nevertheless followed his instincts in a courageous show of character, opposing what he felt could, and indeed did, result from passage of the Tonkin Gulf Resolution. After the introduction of the resolution, Nelson, in a conversation with his legislative assistant, Gar Alperovitz, commented, "Suppose they put in a million men and suppress the V. C. What then? Do we stay forever? Because as soon as we leave, the communists will be back and nothing can prevent that."[18] Alperovitz ultimately drafted the language of the Nelson Amendment[19] during a late night strategy session, August 6, 1964, when the resolution was scheduled for a final vote the next day.[20] As history has proven, Nelson's position became the accepted truth. The administration's policy was a failure, though tragically it took 58,000 American deaths to prove it.

So through the late summer and fall of 1964, into the spring of 1965, before the massive military appropriations bill was passed, the Senate slept and took no action at the early stages when the Vietnam tragedy could yet have been aborted. An understanding of why it was not will be clarified in the following chapters.

NOTES

1. Senator Aiken served in the U.S. Senate from January 10, 1941, until he retired in 1975. He was a very close friend of Senator Mike Mansfield (D.-Mont.), the majority leader during the Johnson years. Indeed, for years they ate breakfast together in the Senate staff cafeteria. See George D. Aiken, *Aiken Senate Diary, January 1972–January 1975* (Brattleboro, Vt.: Stephen Greene Press, 1976).

2. Michael Beschloss, *Taking Charge: The Johnson White House Tapes, 1963–64* (New York: Simon and Schuster, 1997), p. 258.

3. Senator Russell took his Senate seat in January 1933, at the beginning of Franklin Roosevelt's first term. He remained in the Senate until his death in 1971. He was chairman or ranking minority member of the Armed Services Committee for many years.

4. Arthur Schlesinger, Jr., *A Thousand Days* (Boston: Houghton Mifflin, 1964), p. 140.

5. Lee Powell, *J. Wm. Fulbright and America's Lost Crusade* (Little Rock, Ark.: Rose Publishing, 1984), p. 85.

6. See Prologue.

7. Herbert V. Schandler, *The Unmaking of a President* (Princeton, N.J.: Princeton University Press, 1977), pp. 43–45.

8. David Halberstam, *The Best and the Brightest* (New York: Random House, 1969), p. 305.

9. Ibid., p. 645. It likely refers to the May 19, 1967, memo from McNamara to LBJ recommending a change in fundamental U.S.-Vietnam policy. *See also* Robert McNamara *In Retrospect* (New York: Random House, 1995), pp. 233–37.

10. Interview with Senator Gaylord Nelson, May 2, 1996.

11. Doris Kearns Goodwin, *No Ordinary Times* (New York: Simon and Schuster, 1994), p. 278.

12. Robert F. Kennedy, *Thirteen Days* (Signet ed., New York: W. W. Norton, 1969), p. 54.

13. Elie Abel, *The Missile Crisis* (Bantam ed., London: Mac Gibbon and Kee, 1966), p. 102.

14. McNamara, *In Retrospect*, p. 341.

15. Senator Morse was a native of Dane County, Wisconsin. Further discussion of his background and career can be found in Chapter 2.

16. Cong. Rec. S8159 (Daily ed., July 28, 1945).

17. Interview with Senator Gaylord Nelson, May 2, 1996.

18. Ibid.

19. See text of Nelson Amendment in Chapter 3.

20. Interview with Senator Gaylord Nelson, May 2, 1996.

BACKGROUND TO THE PASSAGE OF S.J. 189

The Senator [Richard Russell] said to newsmen: "The U.S. made a terrible mistake getting involved in Vietnam."[1]

The first American influence in the Vietnam War was felt in 1950 when the United States began to finance the French against the communist Viet Minh.[2] By 1954 the exhausted French were nearing final defeat in their eight-year struggle. As the garrison at Dien Bien Phu neared collapse and ultimate surrender in May 1954, American supporters of the French urged American air strikes.[3] Admiral Arthur Radford, Chairman of the Joint Chiefs of Staff, and Secretary of State John Foster Dulles, together with Vice President Richard Nixon urged U.S. air support for the French.

The Eisenhower administration floated a trial balloon stating it was the U.S. intention to send two combat divisions, after having sent forty B-26 bombers and two hundred advisors in February 1954. Immediate Senate opposition caused the administration to announce withdrawal of the advisors by June 12, 1954, and Majority Leader William Knowland (R.-Cal.) stated on the Senate floor that we had no intention to send combat forces.[4]

Senator Richard Russell warned that any U.S. involvement was a mistake that could bring us piecemeal into the war. This was the first of Senator Russell's rare public comments on the Vietnam War. His private opposition was consistent until his death in 1971. Despite his role as leading Democratic military spokesman and later Chairman of the Armed Services Committee, Senator Russell never made public his true feelings of opposition to U.S. involvement in Vietnam. Yet he was the one senator whose integrity, power, and prestige could have halted the war quickly.[5]

Years later, in spring 1965, at LBJ's urging, Dwight Eisenhower's advice was that since the United States had "appealed to force" in Vietnam, therefore "we have got to win."[6] Similarly in his January 19, 1961 conference with President-elect John F. Kennedy, Ike said in reference to Laos, "You might have to go in there and fight it out."[7]

This, however, was not the position of President Eisenhower in 1954 when he was in power and vetoed any U.S. military action in Vietnam. He stated on February 10, 1954, "No one could be more bitterly opposed to ever getting the United States in a hot war in that region than I am." He further stated that he could not "conceive of a greater tragedy for America than to get heavily involved now in an all out war in any of those regions, particularly with large units."[8]

Later, on April 3, 1954, at Eisenhower's behest, Dulles, representing the interventionists, together with Arthur Radford, met with Senators Russell and Lyndon B. Johnson, Senate minority leader. Radford spoke for air strikes and was supported by Senator Knowland, the Senate majority leader, Senator Earle Clements of Kentucky, a ringer Eisenhower brought in with loaded questions, asked Radford if the other chiefs were in agreement with him and if so how many. Radford replied "none." After Senator Johnson argued against Admiral Radford's position Army Chief of Staff General Matthew B. Ridgway, a World War II hero, and former commander of UN forces in the Korean War, spoke. He said that air power without ground support was useless and predicted almost prophetically that intervention would require from 500,000 to 1,000,000 troops. After reporting to President Eisenhower, who had shrewdly orchestrated the meeting and Ridgway's appearance, Ridgway would write, "The idea of intervening was abandoned."[9] This episode is in dramatic contrast with the actions of President Johnson.

President Johnson, at the outset, also had severe misgivings concerning involvement in an Asian land war. In a conversation on February 3, 1964, LBJ recalled, "Well, I opposed it in '54 [intervention in Vietnam]. But we're there now."[10] But, despite his consummate skill as a legislator, he could not avoid the manipulation and persuasion of Robert McNamara, McGeorge Bundy, and the rest. They forced his hand.

Eisenhower, it is now clear, did just the opposite. He was able to force the advisors to comply with his basic wish to avoid war. The manner in which he carried this off was through a degree of political sophistication worthy of FDR himself. Johnson allowed his options to be foreclosed early on, while Eisenhower, with his huge prestige, held his options open. Thus, we see that when he was younger and the burden of responsibility was upon him, President Eisenhower's approach to military involvement in southeast Asia was quite different from that of later years. President Kennedy's stated position was not to impose American or Western control and power in southeast Asia. Rather, his policy aimed toward neutrality in the region. Neutrality of course precluded force of arms by one state against another.[11] Nevertheless, during his term of office approximately 16,000 United States advisors, including military personnel, were sent to South Vietnam. It was not yet clear what the purpose of these advisors really was.[12]

During the Kennedy years, contact between U.S. and North Vietnamese troops was frequent; casualties were suffered. It will be shown that the United States did not have completely clean hands during these events. Although the French had fought Ho Chi Minh for eight years and had sustained 240,000 casualties, the danger of U.S. involvement in the same battle began to increase, despite Senator Russell's warning of piecemeal entry into the war.

Despite Lyndon Johnson's opposition to American involvement in Vietnam in 1954, the world had changed by 1964. He was now the new president, and contradictory pressures were brought upon him. Perhaps as a way of testing the new president, whose complex character and views were not really known, the Joint Chiefs of Staff sent a memo to LBJ in January 1964 which would have the United States put aside self-imposed restrictions "and to undertake bolder action which may embody greater risks."[13] This call for escalation and provocation was more than half a year before the Gulf of Tonkin incidents.

In Saigon, during early 1964, it became clear that the generals who came to power through the coup against Diem, meaning Generals Dvong Van Minh, Tran Van Don, and Tran Van Kim, were ineffective.[14]

For the time being, President Johnson withstood the pressures of the military. He was torn by indecision in early 1964. On February 3, 1964, he asked John Knight, Chairman of the Board of the *Miami Herald*, "What do you think we ought to do in Vietnam?" Knight replied, "I never thought we belonged there. . . . I think President Kennedy thought at one time that we were overcommitted in that area."[15] But later at the critical period, despite his misgivings, LBJ was not able to withstand the pro-war pressures building against him. In June 1964, General Paul D. Harkins was replaced by General William Westmoreland as commander of U.S. advisory personnel in Vietnam. General Westmoreland was a more competent, respected military leader.[16]

In February 1965, General Harold Johnson, Army Chief of Staff, told LBJ that Vietnam could be Korea all over, only worse. Yet a month later he recommended sending up to four divisions of U.S. combat troops to

Vietnam.[17] In May 1964, Senator Russell clearly told LBJ of his fears of another Korea. "It frightens me 'cause it's my country and if we get in there on any considerable scale, there's no doubt in my mind that the Chinese will be in there and . . . it'd be a Korea on a much bigger scale." President Johnson replied, "You don't have any doubt, but what if we go in there and get 'em up against the wall. The Chinese communists are gonna come in?" Russell answered, "No doubt about it," and LBJ agreed, "That's my judgment, and our people don't think so."[18]

Later, in July 1965, General Westmoreland's increased troop request, although enthusiastically supported by Bundy, raised LBJ's fears of a new Korea in the making. Between receipt of Westmorland's cable and the final decision, Johnson challenged his advisors, "Where are we heading, is this another Korea?"[19] General Johnson's February warning had obviously struck home.

Most significant of all is the political background against which the events of August 1964 were occurring. Johnson was, at the time, in the beginning of his presidential campaign against Senator Barry Goldwater (R.-Ariz.). Johnson was fearful of Goldwater. On August 3, 1964, Robert Anderson, a conservative Republican and former Secretary of the Treasury under Eisenhower, told LBJ, "You're going to be running against a man who's a wild man on this subject."[20]

Johnson expressed these fears even earlier, in February 1964, when he told an acquaintance, "[w]hat they said about us leaving China would just be warming up, compared to what they would say now. I see Nixon is raising hell about it today. Goldwater, too."[21] The Democrats sought to paint Goldwater into the corner as an extremist. His loose remarks made their job easier. As an example, Goldwater stated that LBJ's admonition to naval commanders during the crisis told them to use "any weapons necessary."[22] This was in response to a question at a press conference in Hershey, Pennsylvania, as to whether he felt Johnson had authorized use of nuclear weapons. Goldwater's remarks were vehemently and gleefully attacked by McNamara and Dean Rusk as "both unjustified and irresponsible."[23]

Senator J. William Fulbright later said that he had not been "in a suspicious frame of mind" about Johnson's intentions, but "I was afraid of Goldwater."[24] LBJ, too, was fearful of Goldwater. A request of McNamara revealed both the president's concern about Goldwater's reactions and his own doubts of what U.S. policy really was. On August 3, Johnson said to McNamara, "Now I wish that you'd give me some guidance on what we ought to say. . . . The people . . . want to be damned sure I don't . . . cut and run. That's what all the country wants because Goldwater is raising so much hell about how he's gonna blast 'em off the moon."[25]

S.J. 189 permitted Johnson to wrap himself in the flag, to deflect right-wing Republican challenges to his patriotism. Despite the fact that Johnson had no idea what his ultimate policy would be, through S.J. 189 he showed himself to be alert toward any danger to American forces, but moderate in tone and in action. Without a clear plan in mind, LBJ, the old Senate master, wanted congressional support whichever way he turned.

Indeed, when S.J. 189 came to the Senate on August 5, 1964, Senator Fulbright told Senator George McGovern, "Look, Lyndon wants this, there's nothing dangerous in it or I wouldn't be sponsoring this."[26] Johnson's campaign theme was, as he said in an Akron, Ohio, speech on October 21, that Asian boys must fight Asian wars.[27]

In later months, Senator Fulbright told Senator Gaylord Nelson, an early opponent of the Gulf of Tonkin resolution, that the resolution "was sort of a cheerleader's resolution, that the President wanted something passed that looked like it gave him authority to respond with significant massive retaliation if they didn't behave themselves [so] to speak."[28]

Today, it is clear that Lyndon Johnson did not want an expanded land war in Asia. In early 1965, LBJ, preparing a speech he was to deliver, told McNamara, "I'll tell you what I would say about it. I would say that we have a commitment to Vietnamese freedom. Now we could pull out of there. . . . We could send our Marines in there and we could get tied down in a third world war or another Korean action."[29] The goal of his presidency was to be the Great Society. Senator McGovern told this author that in his opinion if not for the tragic blunder of the war LBJ could have been considered on the domestic front the greatest president in U.S. history.[30]

Nor did the initial supporters of the resolution seem to understand the possibility of the massive war that followed. Senator Russell, Chairman of the Armed Services Committee, stated on the Senate floor on February 28, 1967, during consideration of a military appropriations bill, "But I am frank to say that I didn't expect the war to assume this magnitude at the time we passed the resolution."[31]

Despite the passage of 35 years, it is even more important to understand exactly what happened during those early days in August 1964 in the Gulf of Tonkin and what led to the United States' response. The short remarks of President Johnson quoted in the Prologue were the basic administration version. It was stated in greater detail and clarity by Secretary McNamara at the August 6 hearing.

STATEMENT OF HONORABLE ROBERT S. MCNAMARA, SECRETARY OF DEFENSE

Secretary McNamara. Mr. Chairman, I prepared a statement which is available to members of the committee that outlines the events that led up to the attack of the U.S. forces on August 4. You will recall that our destroyer Maddox operating in international waters was attacked on the 2d: Maddox and the Turner Joy on the 4th and we responded on the 4th, Washington Time.

I would be happy to read this statement, it is seven pages, or answer questions about the details, whichever you choose.

Chairman Fulbright. If you would care to, put it in the record. Most of us have heard the facts but if you could highlight it.

Secretary McNamara. I would be happy to do so.

Three PT boats attacked the Maddox, launched torpedoes against it; Maddox returned fire with her 5-inch guns, believed they destroyed one of the boats, the other two were destroyed either by the Maddox or the carrier Ticonderoga's planes which you can see positioned south of Hainan Island.

I reported on Monday in my briefings to the Congress that I believed this to be an isolated incident, perhaps a miscalculation or misunderstanding by the North Vietnamese, and we did not anticipate it would be repeated.

Contrary to my estimate it was repeated on August 4 at which time between three and six North Vietnamese patrol boats attacked the Maddox and the Turner Joy which had been sent to accompany it on its patrol course.[32]

At this time the vessels were about 60 miles off the coast of North Vietnam. The attack occurred at night. It appeared to be a deliberate attack in the nature of an ambush.

Torpedoes were launched, automatic weapons fire was directed against the vessels. They returned the fire. Aircraft from the Ticonderoga and by this time the Constellation which had been brought down [deleted] to support the Ticonderoga, were sent over the vessels and returned the patrol boat's fire.

We believe that two of the patrol boats were destroyed as a result of the fire. Engagement was broken off after 2 to 3 hours of fire. The meetings in Washington you are familiar with, the following day.

The President decided that this deliberate attack, required a military response. We, therefore, launched in the daylight hours about noon-time local time about midnight on August 5, 12:30 in the morning August 5, against the bases from which these boats had come against the boats themselves, and against certain support facilities, particularly a petroleum depot at Vinh; 64 sorties were directed against these targets. We believe that about 25 boats were damaged or destroyed, certain shore facilities were destroyed. About 90 percent of the Vinh petroleum depot which

contains about 10 percent of the total storage capacity of petroleum in North Vietnam was destroyed.

We think there were very few civilian casualties because these
bases and the depot were in isolated portions of North Vietnam.

Our losses were two aircraft destroyed, two pilots lost, and
two aircraft very slight damaged.

The patrol is being resumed and will continue its normal
course southward in the Gulf of Tonkin.[33]

The full statement of Secretary McNamara is set forth in Appendix
III.[34]

At the August 6 congressional hearings, Secretary McNamara stated
that our ships were "engaged in a routine patrol in International waters."[35] This, too, was the position defended by Senator Fulbright in the
Senate floor debate.

> *Mr. Fulbright.* It has been asserted by others that the Maddox
> was backing up or convoying the smaller vessels of the Vietnam-
> ese. The testimony I am familiar with shows that this is not a
> fact.[36]

Senator Wayne Morse continued to term the United States a provocateur.[37] The U.S. presence in close proximity to the North Vietnamese
shoreline on July 31 was but one example that Senator Morse cited.[38]

After 35 years, the question still remains. Were our ships attacked or
was the entire incident a provocation by the Johnson administration, at
McNamara's urging, to provide an excuse for a show of force in Vietnam?

The SOG (Special Operation Group) was a secret unit comprised of
Seals, Green Berets, and other special forces. Small SOG vessels bom-
barded a coastal radar station on the night of August 3. The incident
that led to the Gulf of Tonkin Resolution occurred August 4. Nevertheless, a former ranking SOG officer contends that SOG did not "lure"
North Vietnam into attacking the *Maddox*. "Hanoi already was committed to wider war."[39]

Senator George McGovern told this author that with the exceptions of
Senators Morse and Ernest Gruening (D.-Alaska), senators did believe
the attacks had occurred, as stated by Johnson's spokesman.[40]

Senator Nelson told this author in the 1996 interview, "I don't know
what the historians have written about the so-called attack upon the ship.
I don't think there was a real attack. But did the President? It comes to
the President and I think he probably did."

Dr. Gar Alperovitz, Senator Nelson's legislative director, who drafted
the Nelson Amendment, didn't believe any attack had taken place.[41] Of

critical importance in the development of this crisis is that McNamara said in his statement of August 6[42] that the *Maddox* was on a routine patrol on the high seas. In his 1995 book, Secretary McNamara writes, "the idea that the Johnson administration deliberately deceived Congress is false. The problem was not that Congress did not grasp the resolution's potential but that it did not grasp the war's potential and how the administration would respond in the face of it."[43]

As we now know, the *Maddox* was really on an intelligence gathering assignment, sailing close to shore and not on routine patrol.[44] Secondly, Congress was given three days to become acquainted with the issue, hearings lasting one hour and forty minutes, with only administration proponents testifying. In that short time, Congress, according to the Secretary, even in his *mea culpa*, was to have grasped or divined the war's potential and how the administration would react. McNamara further states in his book, "Senator Fulbright, in time, came to feel that he had been misled and indeed he had. He had received definite assurances from Dean at the August 6, 1964, hearing (and I believe privately from LBJ as well) that the President would not use the vast power granted him without full congressional consultation."[45]

Was there any substantive proof to throw a shadow over the administration version? Edwin E. Moise has provided the clearest version of what happened in the Gulf of Tonkin in his 1996 work, *Tonkin Gulf and the Escalation of the Vietnam War*. He concludes that the United States did not knowingly falsify the August 4 attack.[46] Today, however, Secretary McNamara writes that he doesn't believe the August 4 incident took place.[47] Thus, his sincerity in the August 6, 1964, testimony is not in question, according to the him.

Prior to publication of these two books, historian Tom Wells had written that as the jets were getting set to carry out the reprisal raids McNamara was informed by Admiral U.S. Grant Sharp, Commander in Chief, Pacific Naval Forces (CINCPAC), that it was now unclear to officers on the spot whether the two U.S. ships had actually been attacked.[48] Wells contends that McNamara ordered the reprisal attacks before Admiral Sharp could get back to him. In early 1965 LBJ is quoted as having said concerning the second attack, "For all I know our Navy was shooting at whales out there."[49]

In yet another version, which rings true, Admiral Thomas Moorer testified in 1970 at the hearing to confirm his appointment as Chairman of the Joint Chiefs of Staff. He testified that the *Maddox* opened fire only after having come under torpedo attack. The Navy history tells that the *Maddox* made a positive identification of the lead Vietnamese warship at 9,800 yards, but that the first Vietnamese torpedo was launched "unobserved by the *Maddox*" between 9,000 and 5,000 yards from the U.S. ship. Since the *Maddox* opened fire at 9,000 yards, it could not have known it was already under attack. Evidence thus indicates that the *Maddox*, if there was an engagement, opened fire first, based upon the approach of the North Vietnamese vessels. Officers aboard the *Turner Joy* have contended that they saw no attacking boats or firing upon the U.S. ship.[50]

In late 1967, a former naval officer, John W. White, wrote a letter to the *New Haven Register* in Connecticut charging that the second attack did not take place. Lieutenant (JG) White was, at the time, aboard a seaplane tender and had access to radio messages on the high command circuit. He wrote, "I recall clearly the confusing radio messages sent at that time by the destroyers, confusing because the destroyers themselves were not certain that they were being attacked."[51]

Such charges were a factor in causing Fulbright to hold open hearings in February 1966 and February 1968 examining the entire history of U.S. participation in the Vietnam War.

In reality the *Maddox* was part of what was known as the DeSoto patrol, U.S. ships especially supplied with electronic equipment for intelligence gathering. McNamara was challenged with this at the 1968 hearings. He denied it, sticking to his original 1964 testimony that the *Maddox* was on routine patrol.

In his memoir, Secretary McNamara describes in detail what the DeSoto patrols were. Actually there were two programs, DeSoto patrols and Plan 34A activities. Plan 34A was composed of boats and aircraft dropping South Vietnamese agents into North Vietnam to conduct sabotage and to gather intelligence as well as to launch hit and run attacks against the North Vietnamese.[52] The DeSoto patrols were part of a global system of electronic reconnaissance carried out by specially equipped U.S. naval vessels. McNamara today admits that he knew long before August 1964 that the 34A operations were essentially worthless.[53] However, the *Maddox* was on a DeSoto patrol.[54]

Secretary McNamara's memoirs directly contradict his 1964 testimony that the *Maddox* was on "routine patrol" and also challenges his contention of never having deliberately deceived the Congress or the people.

In a 1996 meeting, General Vo Nguyen Giap, former Commander of North Vietnamese forces, told Secretary McNamara that the second attack never took place.[55]

It would seem that, at this late date, with many of the principal participants deceased, and others maintaining their old positions, it isn't possible to determine with absolute certainty what happened in the Gulf of Tonkin. It is possible, though, to conclude that the sequence and elements in the administration's version were not true. Whether this was an attempt to deceive or a genuine mistake cannot be judged.

The early acceptance of the administration's version of events, through the fall of 1964, would help account for the fact that senators did not challenge the administration policy. Congress was out of session and senators were out campaigning in their home states. Perhaps an even more important reason for senatorial inactivity was reliance upon LBJ's speech in Akron, Ohio, on October 21 that he had no plans to send American boys to fight Asian wars.[56] He was believed, and a sense of relief affected senators as well as the general public. Senator Olin Johnston (D.-S.C.) told LBJ he had announced that he would vote for the president, saying, "I'm for keeping us out of war and I'm voting for Lyndon Johnson. . . . You are going to find in my state, and in the South, these mothers and people are afraid of war."[57] So apparently there was nothing in the fall of 1964 to be concerned or fearful about. Afterward began the tactics of deceit and lies.

This, in brief, was the historical and current political background from which S.J. 189 emerged.

NOTES

1. *New York Times*, December 31, 1964, p. 4.

2. David Halberstam, *The Best and the Brightest* (New York: Random House, 1969), p. 136.

3. Ibid., p. 137.

4. Ibid., p. 139.

5. Further discussion of Senator Russell's refusal to publicly advocate his private position is in the Introduction.

6. Robert McNamara, *In Retrospect* (New York: Random House, 1995), p. 190.

7. Theodore Sorenson, *Kennedy* (New York: Bantam 1966), p. 722.

8. Dwight D. Eisenhower, *Public Papers of the Presidents of the United States: Dwight D. Eisenhower, 1953–61*, 8 vols. (Washington, D.C.: Government Printing Office, 1960–61), p. 250.

9. Halberstam, *The Best and the Brightest*, pp. 143–44. See also speech by Senator John F. Kennedy on the question of intervention in Vietnam upon the French surrender, Appendix VI.

10. Michael Beschloss, *Taking Charge: The Johnson White House Tapes, 1963–64* (New York: Simon and Schuster, 1997), p. 213.

11. Sorenson *Kennedy*, p. 732.

12. According to Sorenson, the U.S. advisors had trained the South Vietnamese to withstand a Korea-type invasion. As the conflict developed into guerrilla warfare, the U.S. role became less clear. Sorenson, pp. 732–35.

13. Halberstam, *The Best and the Brightest*, p. 350.

14. Ibid., p. 351.

15. Beschloss, *Taking Charge*, p. 213.

16. Halberstam, *The Best and the Brightest*, p. 405.

17. Lloyd Gardner, *Pay Any Price* (Chicago: Ivan R. Dee Publishers, 1995), p. 181.

18. Beschloss, *Taking Charge*, p. 367.

19. Gardner, *Pay Any Price*, p. 220.

20. Beschloss, *Taking Charge*, p. 494.

21. Ibid., p. 213.

22. *New York Times*, August 13, 1964, 1:8.

23. Ibid., 1:5.

24. LeRoy Ashby and Rod Gramer, *Fighting the Odds* (Pullman: Washington State University Press, 1994), p. 184.

25. Beschloss, *Taking Charge*, p. 495.

26. Interview with Senator George McGovern, February 29, 1996.

27. *New York Times*, October 22, 1964.

28. Interview with Senator Gaylord Nelson, May 2, 1996.

29. Beschloss, *Taking Charge*, p. 248.

30. Interview with Senator George McGovern, February 29, 1996.

31. Cong. Rec. S4720 (Daily ed., Feb. 28, 1967).

32. At 11:06 A.M., McNamara informed the President that Admiral Sharp telephoned that the second destroyer is under attack. The President asked, "Now where are these torpedoes coming from?" McNamara replied, "We don't know. Presumably from those unidentified craft that I mentioned to you a moment ago." Beschloss, *Taking Charge*, p. 498.

33. Southeast Asia Resolution joint hearing before the Foreign Relations Committee and the Armed Services Committee, 88th Congress, August 6, 1964, p. 6ff.

34. Ibid., p. 8ff. The full statement by Secretary McNamara is in Appendix III.

35. Southeast Asia hearings, pp. 6–7.

36. Cong. Rec. S18402 (Daily ed., Aug. 6, 1964).

37. Ibid., 18426.

38. Ibid., 18425.

39. John L. Plaster, *The Secret Wars of America's Commandos in Vietnam* (New York: Simon and Schuster, 1997).

40. Interview with Senator McGovern, February 29, 1996.

41. Interview with Dr. Gar Alperovitz, February 13, 1996.

42. Southeast Asia Resolution hearings, p. 7.

43. McNamara, *In Retrospect*, p. 141.

44. See David Wise, "Remember the Maddox" (*Esquire*, April 1968), p. 123.

45. McNamara, *In Retrospect*, p. 141.

46. Edwin E. Moise, *Tonkin Gulf and the Escalation of the Vietnam War* (Chapel Hill: University of North Carolina Press, 1996), p. 203. Further individual accounts of U.S. personnel aboard the *Maddox* and *Turner Joy* are cited on pp. 142–185.

47. McNamara, *In Retrospect*, p. 210.

48. Tom Wells, *The War Within: America's Battle over Vietnam* (Berkeley: University of California Press, 1994) p. 11.

49. Ibid.

50. John Prados, *The Hidden History of the Vietnam War* (Chicago: Ivan Dees Publishing, 1993), pp. 48–53.

51. Prados, *Hidden History of the Vietnam War*, p. 52.

52. McNamara, *In Retrospect*, p. 129.

53. Ibid., p. 131.

54. Ibid. For a detailed description of the DeSoto patrols see Moise, *Tonkin Gulf*, pp. 50–72.

55. *New York Times*, September 19, 1996.

56. *New York Times*, October 22, 1964.

57. Beschloss, *Taking Charge*, p. 501.

2

PASSAGE OF S.J. 189—THE GULF OF TONKIN RESOLUTION

> In wartime truth is so precious that she should always be attended by a bodyguard of lies.[1]
>
> —Winston S. Churchill

AUGUST 5

Accompanied by a message from Lyndon Johnson, the resolution was set before the Senate on August 5. Senator Hubert Humphrey received it, stating that it related to a "grave international situation."

Senator Wayne Morse immediately rose in opposition. His position was that Art. I, §8 of the Constitution which states "The Congress shall have power . . . to declare war," precludes the President from conducting war unilaterally.[2]

Senator Morse beseeched his long-time colleague, Senator J. William Fulbright, to hold regular hearings to explain to the Senate and the public the complexity of the Vietnam issue. Fulbright refused, saying that a state of emergency existed.[3] Others were not able to perceive the emergency.

Senator Morse's position was consistent through the years despite Secretary of State Dean Rusk's questionable comparison of the 1955 Formosa Resolution and the 1957 Mid-East Resolution, both of which Senator Morse had opposed, and the 1962 Cuban Missile Crisis Resolution which he supported. The basic difference between the resolutions was that the 1962 Cuban Resolution did not grant the President unilateral power to wage war. This point will be analyzed in detail in Appendix V.[4]

Wayne Morse had served as Dean of the University of Oregon Law School and was elected to the United States Senate as a Republican in 1944. After re-election in 1950, he quit the Republican party in disillusionment over the policies of President Eisenhower and had become an Independent. In January 1955, he joined the Democratic caucus and was rewarded by Majority Leader Lyndon B. Johnson with a coveted seat on the Senate Foreign Relations Committee, which usually came with long party seniority. By 1956, Senator Morse was a regular Democratic Senator.[5]

Johnson knew of Morse's profound intelligence and legal skill and the damage that Morse's opposition could do to Johnson's position. He referred to Morse as "my lawyer," hoping a bit of flattery might work.[6] Of course, it didn't.

In 1967 when the dissent over the war was a foremost national issue, the country was on the verge of a railway strike. Senator Morse was chairman of the Senate subcommittee on Labor, and the parent Labor and Public Welfare Committee was sitting in executive session when a secretary announced that the President was on the line for Morse. After a bit of kidding that Bob Kennedy should take the call instead, Morse spoke with Johnson and agreed to handle the matter in Congress to legislate a cooling-off period.[7] So even though the two often differed so bitterly over Vietnam, they worked together on other matters with civility and public mutual respect—much in contrast to the publicly personal animosity Johnson held toward J. William Fulbright. Morse's education subcommittee passed all of Johnson's Great Society education bills—the Elementary and Secondary Education bill, Head Start, and the Teacher Corps, among others.

Just as Morse was later more bitter toward Fulbright for going along with Johnson, so too did Johnson despise Fulbright for what he regarded as a betrayal.[8] For Johnson's course of action heretofore was based on Fulbright's agreement and support.

Later, in the last months of his Senate career, Morse became convinced that his phones were tapped, and the personal strain between himself and the President did become public.[9] The recently released Johnson tapes show that, as early as August 7, 1964, Johnson let his private bitterness toward Morse appear. Commenting upon Senator Ernest Gruening, Johnson told Speaker John McCormack, "Oh, he's no good. He's worse than Morse. . . . And Morse is just undependable and erratic as he can be."[10]

In his initial speech on August 5, Senator Morse had already termed the United States a provocateur, claiming that U.S. destroyers acted as backups for South Vietnam naval vessels that were bombarding North Vietnam territory within three to five or six miles of the North Vietnam coast, knowing that both Vietnams recognized a 12-mile territorial boundary at sea.[11]

Throughout this period Senator Morse had access to an early version of "Deep Throat." The source was a Pentagon officer who knew Morse. He called Morse late in the evening and said that since he was in uniform he couldn't reveal specific information, but rather suggested questions Morse should ask Robert McNamara, such as what was the actual mission of the *Maddox*. Asked at the hearing on August 6, McNamara replied that, as he said in his written statement, the ship was on routine patrol.[12] Despite McNamara's later disclaimers, this was one of the first major lies told to the Congress and public by the administration.

Citing the basis for U.S. involvement in an advisory capacity, Morse quoted from the 1954 letter from President Dwight Eisenhower to President Ngo Dinh Diem of South Vietnam that "the government of the United States expects that this aid will be met by performance on the part of the government of Vietnam in undertaking needed reforms."[13]

In a conversation with James Reston of the *New York Times*, LBJ began by asking, "Tell me, what's *your* feeling about Vietnam?" Reston replied, "Oh, I'd just depress you.... I think the Lord will strike me dead for saying anything in favor of Mr. de Gaulle ... but ... France's experience is right. We can't do anything about it without the acquiescence of China." Referring to President Eisenhower's 1954 letter to Diem, President Johnson remarked, "Whether good or bad or whether he was wise or unwise ... I'll help you economically and militarily and spiritually. ... But you'll have to help yourself.... Now not to go in with our own ... ground troops or with our own air. Not to drop atomic bombs and burn the trees. And not to involve China."[14] President Johnson again had revealed his inner doubts and fears of deeper American participation. Tragically, his instincts proved to be correct but his judgment was flawed.

The consistent instability and corruption of the South Vietnamese governments would have provided ample basis later on for U.S. withdrawal. And, interestingly, General William Westmoreland wrote in later years:

> Whether the United States would, in fact, have pulled out of Vietnam in 1965 if the political instability showed no signs of abating is problematical. I think it's likely that Washington was already too deeply committed in word and deed to do other than more of the same. Yet so obvious was the bickering, the machination, the inefficiency, the divisiveness among the Vietnamese that I suspect few in the world would have faulted us at that

point had we thrown up our hands in despair. When we failed to renege on our commitment under such blatantly exigent conditions, the time when we could have withdrawn with some grace and honor had passed.[15]

Senator Morse concluded his first day's speech citing alleged United States violations of Article 2, §4 of the UN Charter, which reads "All members shall refrain in their international relations from the threat or use of force against the territorial integrity or political independence of any state, or in any other manner inconsistent with the purpose of the United Nations." Article 37 of the UN Charter states, "Should the parties to a dispute of the nature referred to in Article 33 fail to settle it by the means indicated in that article, they shall refer it to the Security Council."

AUGUST 6

August 6 was the day of the abbreviated hearing. Having cited Secretary McNamara's testimony earlier,[16] we remain with the last two witnesses, both strong supporters and architects of administration policy. The following is an oral statement from Secretary of State Dean Rusk.[17]

Secretary Rusk. I would like first then to turn specifically to the resolution which is in front of the committees.

I now turn to the specifics of the resolution before you.

The preamble, I believe, speaks for itself. It spells out in the simplest and shortest terms possible the fact of North Vietnamese attacks, their relation to the overall campaign of aggression by North Vietnam, and the purposes and objectives of the United States in Southeast Asia.

As to the operative sections of the resolution, section I declares the approval and support of the Congress for actions, in response to armed attack on U.S. forces, which the President has the authority and obligation to take in his capacity as Commander in Chief.

Turning next to section 2 of the draft resolution, let me make clear at the outset what the resolution does not embrace. It does not cover action to assist any nation not a member of the Southeast Asia Treaty Organization or a protocol state.

You will recall the protocol states were South Vietnam, Cambodia, and Laos. In the case of Cambodia, they have publicly declared they will not utilize their privilege of calling for help as a protocol state under the Southeast Treaty Organization.

In the case of Laos the 1962 accords contained a declaration by the government of Laos they would not call upon any alliance, or group of nations, for assistance.

Therefore, so long as the 1962 accords are in effect, the government of Laos would be barred from calling on that assistance unless the relevant portions of those particular agreements had in fact withered away.

This resolution does not cover any action in support of a nation unless such nation requests it. It does not cover any action to resist aggression that is not Communist in origin. The Southeast Asia Treaty includes a U.S. understanding that is directed solely against "Communist aggression."

The language, "to take all necessary steps, including the use of armed force," is similar to the authority embraced in the Formosa Resolution of 1955, the Middle East Resolution of 1957, and the Cuba Resolution of 1962.

Copies of each of these have been made available to you for comparative purposes. The Formosa Resolution authorized the President "to employ the Armed Forces of the United States."

The Middle East Resolution stated that the United States was "prepared to use armed forces." The nearest parallel to the language of the present resolution is in the first clause of the Cuba Resolution, that the United States is "determined to prevent by whatever means may be necessary, including the use of arms," Cuban subversive activities extending to any part of the hemisphere.[18]

This analogy to the Cuban resolution was completely untrue, but whether the Secretary's misstatement was deliberately false or mistaken is not known. ·

Secretary Rusk had an additional section to his statement.[19]

PRECEDENTS OF SUCH PRESIDENTIAL ACTION

I shall not take your time this morning to review the constitutional aspect of resolutions of this character. I believe it to be the generally accepted constitutional view that the President has the constitutional authority to take at least limited armed action in defense of American national interest; in at least 85 instances, Presidents of the United State have in fact taken such action.

As I have said before, we cannot now be sure what actions may be required. The Formosa Resolution of 1955 was followed by the use of U.S. warships to escort supply convoys to the offshore islands in 1958; the Middle East Resolution was followed by President Eisenhower's sending of troops to Lebanon in 1958; the Cuba Resolution was followed by the well-known events of October 1962.

I do not suggest that any of these actions may serve as a parallel for what may be required in Southeast Asia. There can be no doubt, however, that these previous resolutions form a solid legal precedent for the action now proposed. Such action is required to make the purpose of the United States clear and to protect our national interests.

Mr. Chairman, I would like to add one comment to this statement, and that is that this resolution, and this consultation which the executive and the legislative branches are now having in the course of today, will in no sense be the last contact between the executive and legislative branches on these problems in Southeast Asia. There will continue to be regular consultations not only with the committee but between the President and the Congressional leaders, and on a bipartisan basis. That has been the practice of Presidents in this postwar period.

Therefore, as the Southeast Asia situation develops, and if it develops, in ways which we cannot now anticipate, of course there will be close and continuous consultation between the President and the leaders of the Congress.[20]

The last statement pledging a "close and continuous consultation between the President and the leaders of the Congress" if the situation in Southeast Asia should change also proved false, as Secretary McNamara states in his book, *In Retrospect*. And even were the promise kept, consultation with "leaders of the Congress" still doesn't satisfy Article I, §8. Rusk additionally over the years has twisted his statement repeatedly, that the President can take "at least limited armed action," to use the resolution as a basis for approval of a full scale war.

The questioning of Sec. McNamara continued.

Senator Stennis. Well, the background, what led up to all this. What do you think about the possibility of Red China's direct participation or prompting or indirect, what is your idea?

Secretary McNamara. We see no evidence of their direct participation in the attack. What their counsel may have been from North Vietnam I can't say.

Senator Stennis. You don't have any intelligence on that?

Secretary McNamara. No, sir; we do not.[21]

The question of Chinese involvement has been noted in a bizarre story told by Dr. Li Zhisui, Mao's private physician, in his book *The Private Life of Chairman Mao*.[22] He tells of a trip Chairman Mao had planned to begin on August 10, 1964; the trip was cancelled five days earlier. "Informed that the United States was sending more troops to Vietnam, Mao wanted to stop and monitor the situation, finally deciding to send Chinese soldiers—secretly and wearing Vietnamese uniforms—to fight the United States."

Nowhere else have I found confirmation of this strange version of Chinese participation in the war. At the outset, Secretary McNamara told LBJ that "the reaction [to the August 4 air strike] from North Vietnam and China is slight so far. Less than I would have anticipated."[23]

In the August 6 floor debate, Fulbright presented the facts of what happened in the Gulf of Tonkin which supported the administration's version.[24] Indeed, Senator Mike Mansfield, Senate Majority Leader and later opponent of the war, as a result at this time also expressed support for the President's position. Senator Mansfield on April 25, 1996, years later, in a conversation with Senator Gaylord Nelson, told Nelson that the only reason he voted for the resolution was his reliance upon Fulbright's assurances that the President did not plan a wider war.[25] Fulbright's contention that the United States acted in accordance with Article 51 of the UN Charter permitting acts of self defense in limited retaliation, has become a controversial position.

A crucial point made to this author by Senator George McGovern in a 1996 interview was that, with the exception of senators Morse and Gruening, most other senators did believe that the attacks had occurred as the administration had stated. Senator Nelson told the author in a 1996 interview, "I don't know what the historians have written about the so-called attack upon the ship. I don't think there was a real attack. But did the President? It comes to the President, and I think he probably did."

But aside from those few exceptions, even the senators with reservations as to the extent of retaliation and to further adherence to basic U.S. policy did not ever seriously question that the two destroyers were attacked on the high seas while on routine patrol.

At this point in the debate Fulbright's answer to basically the same questions began to waver. In response to Senator McGovern's statement that "All of us have been puzzled if not baffled as to why a little state such as North Vietnam should seek a deliberate naval conflict with the United States with the overwhelming naval and air power that we have in that area,"[26] Fulbright had no clear answer—"it is dangerous to speculate as to the motives of one's enemies"—but he restated his position that the U.S. destroyers were operating on routine patrol. Others suggested different answers to the question of why a small state would attack a large, powerful one without provocation. *Maddox* Commander John J. Herrick later was quoted as saying "Asiatics . . . they don't think of the consequences the way we do."[27]

When NBC asked Secretary Rusk that same question, he replied, "I haven't been able, quite frankly, to come to a fully satisfactory explanation. There is a great gulf of understanding between that world and our world, ideological in character. They see what we think of as the real world in wholly different terms. Their very processes of logic are different."[28]

Senator Jacob Javits (R.-N.Y.) raised serious and far-reaching policy questions that demonstrated a perceptive grasp of the current situation, but he lacked the facts upon which to decide.

> *Mr. Javits.* I wish to ask a question, and a rather serious one.
>
> I shall support the resolution, because I think we must defend freedom in that area, or else see the balance of a large segment of the population of the world tipped against freedom. The degree of our resistance under the action that may be taken in Southeast Asia, under the resolution, will determine not only future events in Vietnam, but also the freedom of Malaysia, India, Pakistan, and Indonesia, and perhaps even Australia and New Zealand.
>
> My question is this: To the extent that the Senator may know—and be permitted to disclose—are we not implementing the Southeast Asia Collective Defense Treaty? This treaty has eight countries who are parties to it including the United States in the area, the rest in Europe, Australia, and New Zealand, and ourselves. The inclusion of Cambodia, Laos, and Vietnam is by protocol. That is, the protection of the treaty is extended to them, though they are not parties to it.
>
> The question I address to the Senator is this: Are we to assume that the action which the President has taken with respect to reacting to the attack on American vessels is the result of a consultation with our allies who are parties to the Southeast Asia Collective Defense Treaty?[29]
>
> What I wish to know from the Senator first: have we consulted with our allies? Second, what are we to look to from our allies in the way of assistance, aid, comfort, partnership, and the future implementation of the resolution?[30]

Senator Fulbright's basic reply was that the United States was acting unilaterally. First, this particular action was not taken in consultation with the other signatories of the Southeast Asia Treaty. It was an act for which we took the sole responsibility. It had nothing to do with the treaty. The fact that we were present in the area grew, at least in part, out of our obligations under the treaty. That is one of the reasons why we were in the area, and had been for a number of years. But we would have the right to be there without the treaty.[31]

Fulbright later gave Javits assurances that the United States would use all diplomatic and other means to keep SEATO alive through consultations. This assurance he said came from Secretary Rusk.[32]

Though it still is not clear what that answer meant, it certainly was of no help in the American effort in Vietnam. Senator McGovern, in a 1996 interview, recalled that Senator Daniel Brewster (D.-Md.) said "there is something about this that I don't like." On the floor Senator Brewster challenged Fulbright:

Mr. Brewster. I had the opportunity to see warfare not so very far from this area, and it was very mean. I would look with great dismay on a situation involving the landing of large land armies on the continent of Asia. So my question is whether there is anything in the resolution which would authorize or recommend or approve the landing of large American armies in Vietnam or in China.

Mr. Fulbright. There is nothing in the resolution, as I read it, that contemplates it. I agree with the Senator that that is the last thing we would want to do. However, the language of the resolution would not prevent it. It would authorize whatever the Commander in Chief feels is necessary. It does not restrain the Executive from doing it.[33]

Thus, Senator Fulbright conceded that the language of S.J. 189 would not prevent the President from waging war under the enormous power of the resolution.

It is, therefore, apparent that many Senators did have reservations and concerns about the scope of the resolution. But there was to be no time to caucus or to formulate oppositional strategy. The hearings had been a sham; and on this day, August 6, Majority Leader Mansfield obtained, without objection, a unanimous consent agreement to the resolution's consideration. A total of three hours—two hours to Senator Morse on behalf of opponents and a half-hour each to the majority and minority leaders in favor of passage. The vote would take place under the agreement at 1 P.M., August 7.[34]

Further tentative questions were raised, but all were based upon a lack of familiarity with the intricacies of the issues, a reluctance to appear obstructionist, and, worse, to appear unpatriotic.

Granting the truth of what Senator Mansfield told Senator Nelson in

1996,[35] that he acted in total reliance on Fulbright's assurances, it is still difficult to accept the majority leader's assessment. He had read the resolution, his expertise was the Far East, and he had spent years with Johnson in the Senate. Upon careful reading of the *Congressional Record* of those early days, one senses that many senators were groping in the dark. And Senator Fulbright was of no help, in fact he clouded the issues.

Senator Jack Miller, a conservative Republican from Iowa, questioned Fulbright.

> *Mr. Miller.* I also support the resolution. However, there is some phraseology in the resolution which troubles me somewhat. I should like to ask a question about it. On page 2 of the resolution, there is a clause which reads:
>
> That the Congress approves and supports the determination of the President to prevent further aggression.
>
> It is left open. It does not say aggression against whom. It is broad enough so that it could mean aggression against the United States; or aggression against the South Vietnamese government, which I would suggest certainly fits in with the President's determination. . . .
>
> *Mr. Fulbright.* I believe that both are included in that phrase.[36]

The really pointed questioning of whether the resolution provided the President the authority to wage war with retroactive Congressional approval was raised by Senator Gaylord Nelson (D.-Wis.):

> As I understand, the mission of the United States in South Vietnam for the past 10 years, stating it in the negative, has not been to take over the government of South Vietnam, and has not been to provide military forces to do battle in place of South Vietnamese forces. To state it in the positive sense, our mission has been to supply a military cadre for training personnel, and advisory military personnel as well as equipment and material—our objective being to help in the establishment of an independent stable regime. And, if my memory is right, we had about 1,000 troops there the first 5 or 6 years, up to 1960. There are now approximately 16,000 troops there. In addition, it is now proposed that this number be expanded to, I believe, 21,000.
>
> Looking at sentence 6 of the resolution, I understood it to be the position of the Senator from Iowa [Mr. Miller] that Congress is saying to the President that we would approve the use of any might necessary in order to prevent further aggression. Am I to understand that it is the sense of Congress that we are saying to

the executive branch: "If it becomes necessary to prevent further aggression, we agree now, in advance, that you may land as many divisions as deemed necessary, and engage in a direct military assault on North Vietnam if it becomes the judgment of the Executive, the Commander in Chief, that this is the only way to prevent further aggression?"[37]

Nelson had hit the raw nerve. Did §2 of the resolution change the nature of America's former advisory role to one of active participation in the war? The reply was evasive.

> *Mr. Fulbright.* I do not know how to answer the Senator's question and give him an absolute assurance that large numbers of troops would not be put ashore. I would deplore it. And I hope the conditions do not justify it now.
>
> *Mr. Nelson.* We may very well not be able to nor attempt to control the discretion that is vested in the Commander in Chief. But the Joint Resolution is before the Senate, sent to us, I assume, at the request of the Executive Branch.
>
> *Mr. Fulbright.* The Senator is correct.
>
> *Mr. Nelson.* It was sent to the Congress in order to ascertain the sense of the Congress on the question. I intend to support the Joint Resolution. I do not think, however, that Congress should leave the impression that it consents to a radical change in our mission or objective in South Vietnam. That mission there for 10 years, as I have understood it, has been to aid in the establishment of a viable, independent regime which can manage its own affairs, so that ultimately we can withdraw from South Vietnam.
>
> Mr. President, we have been at the task for 10 years. I am not criticizing the original decision to go into South Vietnam. I do not know how long that commitment should be kept in the event we are unable to accomplish our mission. And I would not wish to make a judgment on that question now. But I would be most concerned if the Congress should say that we intend by the Joint Resolution to authorize a complete change in the mission which we have had in South Vietnam for the past 10 years and which we have repeatedly stated was not a commitment to engage in a direct land confrontation with our Army as a substitute for the South Vietnam Army in a war against North Vietnam and possibly China.

Senator Nelson went on to say, "But I am concerned about the Congress appearing to the Executive Branch and the public that we would endorse a complete change in our mission. That would concern me."[38]

Mr. Fulbright, in what was probably an inadvertent misstatement, replied: "I do not interpret the Joint Resolution in that way at all. It strikes me, as I understand it, that the Joint Resolution is quite consistent with our existing mission and our understanding of what we have been doing in South Vietnam for the last 10 years."[39]

TERRITORIAL WATERS ISSUE

Senator Nelson raised a particularly sensitive question in asking Fulbright what distance offshore we recognized in respect to North Vietnam and China. Fulbright responded that three miles is the established principle that we recognize, and went on to say "one of the reasons given for sending the *Maddox* in closer than 12 miles from the shore was that in doing so the action would demonstrate that we do not recognize the 12 mile limit."[40]

This was a confusing admission. In his testimony, Secretary McNamara stated that the assault upon the *Maddox* began when she was 30 miles from the shore.[41]

American insistence on enforcing a three-mile limit is contrary to the limit of between six and twelve miles recognized by virtually all nations.[42] Insistence upon enforcement of a three-mile limit not recognized by most nations, in a delicate, potentially hostile confrontation seems unduly provocative.

Ironically, it was Nick Katzenbach, co-author of a book on the foundation of international law, who, when Under Secretary of State in 1967, asserted that the Gulf of Tonkin Resolution was to be considered the functional equivalent of a declaration of war.[43]

Senator McGovern relates that Katzenbach's remarks were what caused Senator Eugene McCarthy (D.-Minn.) to run against LBJ in the 1968 primaries.[44] But Senator Nelson pressed Fulbright further.

Mr. Nelson. Recognizing as we all do the great sensitivity of all countries, especially enemies or those hostile to each other, what purpose in the promotion of our mission in South Vietnam is served by having our ships to go within 11 miles of the North Vietnam coast?

Mr. Fulbright. This strikes me as a question that raises a difficult problem with which I tried to deal in describing modern war. The Senator refers to the sensitivities of the North Vietnamese. What about the fact that the North Vietnamese have for years been sending in trained personnel, material, guns, and ammunition, to attack their neighbor? Why should the United States be so careful about the sensitivities of North Vietnam? Of course, we were there for the purpose of observation of what went on in the area, because our people felt it necessary as a part of our activities in protecting and helping to protect South Vietnam.

Mr. Nelson. I do suggest—and this is what I do not understand— if patrolling that close has no necessary bearing upon the mission we have insisted we have in South Vietnam, it would seem to me that perhaps it is not the exercise of our best judgment to do it.

To which Fulbright produced no answer. The colloquy ended in a somewhat bitter exchange.

Mr. Nelson. I would conclude by saying that no two situations are comparable, but it would be mighty risky if Cuban PT boats were firing on Florida, for Russian armed ships or destroyers to be patrolling between us and Cuba, 11 miles out. It would be a grave risk for her to be testing our viewpoint about her patrolling that close when Cuban boats were firing on Florida. So the question was whether the patrolling that close was really necessary to the accomplishment of our mission. We are, after all, dealing with the possibility of incinerating the whole world.

Mr. Fulbright. As the Senator from Wisconsin pointed out, Russian ships come within 4 or 5 miles, although not within 3 miles, of our shores.

Mr. Nelson. I referred to the assumption of Cuban boats firing on Florida.

Mr. Fulbright. We are not firing on Cuba, nor they on us. I do not see how the case is analogous. There is a new state of modern warfare that is not orthodox. It is subversion and guerrilla warfare. These people are, for all practical purposes, engaged in a war, without a declaration of war, that is going on between South and North Vietnam.

Mr. Nelson. I have taken enough time. I merely wish to add that it is not quite correct to say that we are not firing on North Vietnam.

Mr. Fulbright. We are not firing on Cuba, I said.

Mr. Nelson. I said assume a situation in which Cuba was firing on the coast of Florida with PT boats. It would be a risky thing for Russia to be out there testing our viewpoint about their patrol within 11 miles of our coast.

Mr. Fulbright. I do not deny that it is risky. The whole operation is risky. It is full of risks.

Mr. Nelson. I hope we do not take risks that are unnecessary for the achievement of an objective that we have asserted to be ours for the past 10 years.[45]

One can see that in those early days Senator Fulbright was not merely a supporter of administration policy, but was a true believer. Others harbored doubts, such as Senator John Sherman Cooper (R.-Ky.):

Mr. Cooper. I ask these questions for two reasons: One is to get the opinion of the Chairman of the Foreign Relations Committee and of the Chairman of the Armed Services Committee as to the extent of the powers that are given to the President under the resolution. The second is to distinguish between a situation in which we act in defense of our own forces, in which without question we would risk war, and the commitment to defend South Vietnam.

Mr. Fulbright. That is correct.

Mr. Cooper. In that case, or course, we confirm the power that the President now has to defend our forces against an immediate attack.

Mr. Fulbright. The Senator is a very distinguished lawyer, and I therefore hesitate to engage in a discussion with him on the separation of powers and the powers of the President. We are not giving to the President any powers he has under the Constitution as Commander in Chief. We are in effect approving of his use of the powers that he has. That is the way I feel about it.[46]

But despite the substantial number of senators raising critical questions, there was no time for them to meet or agree upon any course of action. The administration was blowing the resolution by the senate before any significant opposition could coalesce.

Senator E. L. Bartlett (R.-Alaska) spoke out.

Mr. Bartlett. I have had deep doubts about the wisdom of our policy in Indochina, with particular reference to Vietnam. I have expressed those doubts many times on the floor of the Senate and elsewhere.

I have feared that there might be an escalation of the war, but I never dreamed that its possibility would come from such causes as have been noted during the past several days.

Mr. President, it has seemed to me that the basic need—that of inspiring the people of South Vietnam to fight for their freedom, bring into being a government of stability, a government that would be free of communist influence—has been too often lacking, despite the massive help that we have given in that far off land.

But he concluded his remarks with "All Americans must unite behind their President."[47] Perhaps a longer debate and time for consideration would have shown him that his initial instincts were correct.

AUGUST 7

Senator Morse began the final day's proceedings by again distinguishing the 1962 Cuba Resolution, which he had supported, from the resolutions of the Gulf of Tonkin, Formosa in 1965, and the Mid-East in 1957, which he said were all constitutionally defective.[48]

Pointing to language in S.J. 189 authorizing the President "to repel any armed attack against the United States," the senior Senator from Oregon questioned "does that mean that the attack must have started or does it mean that all the President and his advisors have to conclude is that in all probability an attack may be made?"

This is preventive war. There is no power in the Constitution for the President to wage a preventive war.[49] Both the conservative *National Review* and liberal *New Republic* in August 1964 termed the solution a "blank check" for the President.

Similar skeptical views were expressed by Senator George Aiken (R.-Vt.), a long time friend of LBJ. Aiken was a wise man. His lack of enthusiastic support bothered Johnson.[50]

> *Mr. Aiken.* Mr. President, for some months it has appeared to me that an expansion of military operations in Southeast Asia was inevitable. I have been skeptical of the repeated assurances of high government officials that no such expansion was contemplated.
>
> I have repeatedly stated to those officials including the President of the United States that I was opposed to an expansion of the war.
>
> The decision, however, was not mine to make. The decision and also the responsibility for expanding such military operations, rest squarely with the President under the authority delegated to him by the Congress over the years.
>
> The President has now made such a decision and has assumed the responsibility.
>
> *Mr. President.* I am still apprehensive over the outcome of his decision. But, since it has been made, I feel that I, as an American

citizen, can do no less than support the President in his capacity as leader of our nation.

I believe that our country will be in greater jeopardy if we do not now support his decision.

I sincerely hope that the fears I have entertained over the past few months may prove to have been groundless. I sincerely hope that the President's action, taken evidently in the belief that vigorous action now will save more lives than it will cost, will prove to be correct.

Mr. President, I shall support the joint resolution even though I still regard the decision of President Johnson with misgivings. It is a very difficult decision to make, but I do not believe that any of us can afford to take a position opposing the President of the United States for exercising the power which we, under our form of government and through our legislative bodies, have delegated to his office.[51]

But Senator Aiken, despite his long years of public service, never really understood what was his duty as a senator. Congress has power aside from the executive power. "Under our form of government and through our legislative bodies, have delegated to his office" is precisely not what our form of government is.

That the judiciary may overrule the executive is something each first-year law student is taught in *Marbury v. Madison*.[52] Yet, members of the United States Senate, after a history of close to 200 years, still did not realize the independence of the legislative branch and the duty of its members to exercise that independence if they think executive action to be wrong. Certainly some senators were vaguely aware of the existence of such power, as in the ability of the Senate to impeach a president. But they did not appear to realize its imposition of a day to day duty to fulfill that responsibility.

With time running out under the unanimous consent agreement,[53] Senator Gaylord Nelson (D.-Wis.) became the only senator during the entire three days of debate to attempt to clarify by amendment precisely what the scope and intent of S.J. 189 was, and to create a legislative history that would eliminate the necessity of reliance on Senator Fulbright's vague and contradictory answers to questions from senators over the past three days.

Nelson pointed out the futility of involvement by citing the American revolution when "even the greatest power on earth couldn't suppress a bunch of untrained soldiers, you know, civilians with a few guns in a revolution."[54] Nelson began by describing the different interpretations senators attributed to S.J. 189, and declared the need for an amendment which would state clearly the resolution's meaning as Senator Fulbright had explained it to Nelson the day before.

Mr. Nelson. Mr. President, I have read the Record. There was some colloquy on the floor yesterday. I noticed that every Senator who spoke had his own personal interpretation of what the Joint Resolution means.

One Senator yesterday stated for the Record that he understands the resolution to mean that there will be no more privileged sanctuaries.

Another Senator interprets the resolution to mean that it would authorize the Chief Executive to eliminate any aggression, future and present. Some Senators interpret this language to mean aggression against South Vietnam; others interpret it to mean aggression directly against our military forces.

Another Senator interpreted the Joint Resolution to mean that it is the sense of Congress that no change is suggested by Congress in the present mission in South Vietnam—the mission that has been ours for 10 years, which is to supply advisers, technical advice, and material, for the purpose of attempting to encourage the establishment of an independent, viable regime, so that we can withdraw our forces; and that it has not been our mission in the past 10 years to substitute our military forces for the South Vietnamese forces, nor to join with them in a land war, nor to fight their battle for them, nor substitute our government for theirs.

This 10-year-old limited mission can be legitimately defended as responsibility of ours to assist free and independent nations; and it can be legitimately questioned, too, because of the geographic location of that mission.

In any event, I am most disturbed to see that there is no agreement in the Senate on what the Joint Resolution means. I would like to see it clarified. I have great confidence in the President. However, my concern is that we in Congress could give the impression to the public that we are prepared at this time to change our mission and substantially expand our commitment. If that is what the sense of Congress is, I am opposed to the resolution. I therefore ask the distinguished Senator from Arkansas if he would consent to accept an amendment, a copy of which I have supplied him. I shall read it into the Record: "(b) the Congress also approves and supports the efforts of the President to bring the problem of peace in Southeast Asia to the Security Council of the United Nations, and the President's declaration that the

United States, seeking no extension of the present military conflict, will respond to provocation in a manner that is 'limited and
fitting.' Our continuing policy is to limit our role to the provision
of aid, training assistance, and military advice and it is the sense
of Congress that, except when provoked to a greater response,
we should continue to attempt to avoid a direct military involvement in the Southeast Asian conflict."

This amendment is not an interference with the exercise of the
President's constitutional rights. It is merely an expression of the
sense of Congress. Would the Senator accept the amendment?

In what he later conceded was one of the greatest mistakes of his
career, Fulbright refused to accept the amendment.[55]

Mr. Fulbright. It states fairly accurately what the President has
said would be our policy, and what I stated my understanding
was as to our policy; also what other Senators have stated. In
other words, it states that our response should be appropriate
and limited to the provocation, which the Senator states as "respond to provocation in a manner that is limited and fitting,"
and so forth. We do not wish any political or military bases
there. We are not seeking to gain a colony. We seek to insure
the capacity of these people to develop along the lines of their
own desires, independent of domination by communism.[56]

The Senator has put into his amendment a statement of policy
that is unobjectionable. However, I cannot accept the amendment
under the circumstances. I do not believe it is contrary to the
Joint Resolution, but it is an enlargement. I am informed that the
House is now voting on this resolution. The House Joint Resolution is about to be presented to us. I cannot accept the amendment and go to conference with it, and thus take responsibility
for delaying matters.

I do not object to it as a statement of policy. I believe it is an
accurate reflection of what I believe is the President's policy,
judging from his own statements. That does not mean that as a
practical matter I can accept the amendment. It would delay matters to do so. It would cause confusion and require a conference
and present us with all the other difficulties that are involved in
this kind of legislative action. I regret that I cannot do it, even
though I do not at all disagree with the amendment as a general
statement of policy.

Mr. Nelson. Judging by the Record of yesterday, many Senators
do not interpret the resolution in the same way.

Mr. Fulbright. Senators are entitled to have different views. However, most members of the committee, with one to two exceptions, interpret it the same way.

The Presiding Officer. The time of the Senator from Wisconsin has expired.

It's not easy to play the "what if" game. Let's imagine that Fulbright would not have so blundered. Would Johnson have later conducted his policy differently? I doubt that even with Nelson's amendment, LBJ would not have cited the resolution as his source of congressional support and would have evaded the plain words of the resolution. But the record would have been clearly against such action.

At a conference on Vietnam policy held October 21, 1967, Senator Nelson recalled the Gulf of Tonkin debate and his resolution which Fulbright then had refused to accept. In the October 21 speech Senator Nelson said: "I was assured that the sense of my amendment was embodied in the resolution, that this was the Administration's own interpretation of the resolution. I was urged to withdraw my resolution to avoid the necessity for a conference between the Senate and House on two versions of the resolution."

Although it is true that these assurances came from a man who today is identified as a critic of Johnson administration policies—Senator Fulbright—in the summer of 1964 he was the administration's official spokesman on this issue. He was manager of the Gulf of Tonkin Resolution on the Senate floor. His words were accepted by everyone as faithfully representing the views of the administration, with which he remained in daily contact.

It is even more impressive to speculate on what would have happened if Senator Fulbright had responded differently. What if he had said, in response to Senator Nelson's questions during the August 7 debate: "This resolution would allow the administration to decide hereafter whatever steps are necessary in Vietnam. It could be used to justify sending hundreds of thousands of American combat troops to Vietnam, and the launching of massive American air attacks on North Vietnam, right up to the border of China."

Senator Fulbright would have been the most repudiated man in American history. The administration would have disavowed every word he uttered, for they could have echoed the statements being made by the opposition in the campaign, and they would have shocked the American public.

Secretary Rusk says today, "There was no question in anyone's mind as to the meaning of the Gulf of Tonkin Resolution. And he is absolutely correct. The Senate and the public were assured, and the administration stood behind those assurances, that the resolution was NOT intended as authorization for escalation of the war."

Refusal to accept the amendment, no doubt orchestrated by the White House, was the first great mistake in the Senate's failure to exercise its constitutional duty to oversee executive policy.

The Nelson amendment was drafted during a late night working session at Nelson's Senate office. The draft was not completed until early in the norming of August 7, the day of the vote. Gar Alperovitz, Nelson's legislative director, drafted the actual language, but the impetus for the desire to limit Johnson's request came from Nelson himself.

It is little known that among the early "doves" were World War II combat heroes such as Senator Nelson who fought in the South Pacific. Senator McGovern had an incredible record of bravery as a bomber pilot in Europe. Alperovitz's main job was to produce language which would be tough enough to accomplish Nelson's desire to prevent use of combat troops, but flexible enough to attract possible recruiting among senators. It did not work out that way.

S.J. 189 passed by a vote of 88–2, Senators Morse and Gruening voting "no." Senators such as Nelson, McGovern, and Frank Church voted "aye" through misplaced faith in the assurance of Fulbright and the administration.

In 1971, Congress repealed the Gulf of Tonkin Resolution.[57] After the Tet offensive of early 1968, Johnson asked Rusk if it was adequate to proceed under the authority of S.J. 189 or should he ask Congress for a declaration of war. Rusk, doubting Congress would support such a declaration, gave Johnson no definitive answer.

SENATOR FULBRIGHT

J. William Fulbright was the single senator most responsible for passage of S.J. 189. Besides his prestigious position of Chairman of the Foreign Relations Committee, his close friendship with President Johnson gave his assurances that the resolution did not contemplate an expanded war profound credibility. In the introduction to this book,[58] examples of Fulbright's flawed and contradictory judgment in the Cuban matter were briefly discussed.

His contradictory behavior over Vietnam was far more serious and raises questions far more difficult to resolve—how the administration's foremost and most enthusiastic supporter turned and became one of its most bitter opponents, in both cases utilizing the prestige and reputation of the Chairman of the Foreign Relation Committee. His support of Johnson's policy did not yield quickly. In mid-March 1965, after the massive Rolling Thunder bombing had begun, Fulbright, on "Meet the Press," expressed his conviction that the air raids were necessary.[59] This came after the Reston column of February 14[60] which stated, "This country is in an undeclared and unexplained war in Vietnam. . . . But the fact is that we are in a war that is not only undeclared and unexplained, but that has not even been debated in the Congress or the country."

Fulbright's position was, as late as March 1965, the most extreme of any of the administration's supporters. Was he really the brilliant scholar his subsequent beatification made him out to be? It would rather appear that he was truly a lightweight, open to manipulation at best and susceptible to false praise at worse.

He had the courage to vote against appropriations for Joe McCarthy's witch hunting committee, standing alone as one of the first to speak out, together with Senator Margaret Chase Smith (R.-Maine). But he could yet also display such enormous naivete and lack of vision on the question of Vietnam. Indeed, Fulbright was frequently the subject of bitter personal ridicule by LBJ, which never happened to Senator Russell or Senator Morse.

Despite his support for international stability based on law and his creation of the Fulbright Scholarship program to increase understanding among people, he nevertheless, in 1956, signed with other southern Senators the "Southern Manifesto" which attacked the Supreme Court's holding in the *Brown* school desegregation case, thus aligning himself with Eastland of Mississippi and the hoodlums of the White Citizens Councils. One constituent wrote to him: "Is this the end of the road for a Rhodes Scholar?"[61]

In 1946, after Truman became President upon FDR's death, there was no vice president at that time under the Constitution. After the Republicans captured both houses of Congress in 1946, Fulbright suggested that the President be of their party and that Taft or Vandenberg be named Secretary of State by Truman, who would then resign the presidency and the Secretary of State, being next in the line of succession, would become President. President Truman's response to this bizarre suggestion was the famous quote in which he referred to Fulbright as that "overeducated Oxford S.O.B."

Fulbright's apprehension that he had made a terrible mistake began when William Westmoreland requested a gradual buildup to 300,000 troops. At first his fears were expressed privately,[62] yet he still believed Johnson to be the force of moderation within the administration. In mid-June 1965, just weeks before U.S. ground troops were introduced, Johnson asked Fulbright to make a public statement of support for his policy. LBJ pleaded that he needed to fight off the hardliners and get to negotiations, to which Fulbright responded with a statement that the President was showing "steadfastness and statesmanship" in his Southeast Asia policy.

Yet in a July 27 meeting in Senator Mansfield's office, Fulbright found a consensus among those present, Senators Russell, John Sparkman (D.-Ala.),[63] Aiken, and Cooper that "insofar as Vietnam is concerned we are deeply enmeshed in a place where we ought not to be; that the situation is rapidly going out of control and every effort should be made to extricate ourselves."[64]

Although Senators Russell and John Stennis had advocated the bombing initially, at the July 27 meeting they agreed it had been a mistake and that Vietnam was of only marginal strategic importance to the United States. These views were expressed in a letter to LBJ. None of the participants spoke out publicly. They did not wish to publicly align themselves with outspoken opponents such as Senators Nelson, McGovern, Morse, and Gruening.

In reply, Johnson brought the senators to the White House and told them there was to be no turning back and that the war might last six or seven years.[65]

The July 27 meeting was a major point of no return. Those present were the core of the Senate establishment. These were not the dissidents as Morse, Nelson, Church, and McGovern. These were senators who had known Johnson and had worked with him for years. Yet they, too, saw disaster coming, that the bombing was a mistake, and that Vietnam was of little strategic value to us. Still, all they did was send a letter—no statements on the Senate floor, no press conferences, no appearances on "Meet the Press."

At this point, J. William Fulbright finally realized that he had been had.

NOTES

1. Winston Churchill, *In Memoriam* (New York: Bantam Books, 1965), p. 156.

2. The full language of S.J. 189 is set forth in Appendix II, and is taken from Cong. Rec. S518133 (Daily ed., Aug. 5, 1964).

3. David Halberstam, *The Best and the Brightest* (New York: Random House, 1969), p. 715.

4. See analysis in Appendix V.

5. U.S. Congress, *Biographical Directory of the United States Congress, 1774–1989* (Washington, D.C.: Government Printing Office, 1989), p. 1541.

6. Halberstam, *The Best and the Brightest*, p. 404.

7. Author was present.

8. Halberstam, *The Best and the Brightest*, p. 429.

9. Lloyd Gardner, *Pay Any Price* (Chicago: Ivan R. Dee Publishers, 1995), p. 164.

10. Michael Beschloss, *Taking Charge: The Johnson White House Tapes, 1963–64* (New York: Simon and Schuster, 1997), p. 508.

11. Cong. Rec. S18134 (Daily ed., Aug. 5, 1964).

12. Anthony Austin, *The President's War* (New York: J. B. Lippincott, 1971), p. 68.

13. The full text of President Eisenhower's letter is as follows (released October 25, 1954, dated October 1, 1954):

Dear Mr. President:

I have been following with great interest the course of developments in Viet-Nam, particularly since the conclusion of the conference at Geneva. The implications of the agreement concerning Viet-Nam have caused grave concern regarding the future of a country temporarily divided by an artificial military grouping, weakened by a long and exhausting war and faced with enemies without and by their subversive collaborators within.

Your recent requests for aid to assist in the formidable project of the movement of several hundred thousand loyal Vietnamese citizens away from areas which are passing under a *de facto* rule and political ideology which they abhor, are being fulfilled. I am glad that the United States is able to assist in this humanitarian effort.

We have been exploring ways and means to permit our aid to Viet-Nam to be more effective and to make a greater contribution to the welfare and stability of the Government of Viet-Nam. I am, accordingly, instructing the American Ambassador to Viet-Nam to examine with you in your capacity as Chief of Government, how an intelligent program of American aid given directly to your government can serve to assist Viet-Nam in its present hour of trial, *provided that your government is prepared to give assurances as to the standards of performance it would be able to maintain in the event such aid were supplied.*

The purpose of this offer is to assist the government of Viet-Nam in developing and maintaining a strong, viable state, capable of resisting attempted subversion or aggression through military means. *The government of the United States expects that this aid will be met by performance on the part of the government of Viet-Nam in undertaking needed reforms.* It hopes that such aid, combined with your own continuing efforts, will contribute effectively toward an independent Viet-Nam endowed with a strong government. *Such a government would, I hope, be so responsive to the nationalist aspirations of its people, so enlightened in purpose and effective in performance, that it will be respected both at home and abroad* and discourage any who might wish to impose a foreign ideology on your free people.

Sincerely,
DWIGHT D. EISENHOWER

His Excellency Ngo Dinh Diem
President of the Council of Ministers
Saigon, Viet-Nam

Emphasis added. Dwight D. Eisenhower, *Public Papers of the Presidents* (Washington, D.C.: Government Printing Office, 1960–61), No. 306, 1954.

14. Beschloss, *Taking Charge*, p. 414.

15. Gardner, *Pay Any Price*, p. 164.

16. As discussed in Chapter 1.

17. Southeast Asia Resolution, pp. 2–6, see Appendix II.

18. Ibid., p. 11.

19. Secretary Rusk's full statement is in Appendix IV.

20. Southeast Asia Resolution, p. 3.

21. Robert McNamara, *In Retrospect* (New York: Random House, 1995), p. 123.

22. Dr. Li Zhisui, *The Private Life of Chairman Mao* (New York: Random House, 1994), p. 123.

23. Beschloss, *Taking Charge*, p. 504.

24. Cong. Rec. S18399 (Daily ed., Aug. 6, 1964).

25. Interview with Senator Gaylord Nelson, May 2, 1996.

26. Cong. Rec. S18420 (Daily ed., Aug. 6, 1964).

27. Gardner, *Pay Any Price*, p. 135.

28. Ibid.

29. Cong. Rec. S18402 (Daily ed., Aug. 6, 1964).

30. Ibid., 18404.

31. Ibid., and 18405.

32. Cong. Rec. S18403 (Daily ed., Aug. 6, 1964).

33. Ibid., 18422.

34. Cong. Rec. S18405–6 (Daily ed., Aug. 6, 1964).

35. Interview with Senator Gaylord Nelson, May 2, 1996.

36. Cong. Rec. S18407 (Daily ed., Aug. 6, 1964).

37. Ibid.

38. Ibid.

39. Ibid.

40. Hearings on Southeast Asia Resolution, Cong. Rec. S18409 (Daily ed., Aug. 6, 1964). Fulbright states that the first attack was when within 25 miles offshore and the second from 60 miles. Senator Richard Russell stated the distances as 30 and 60 miles.

41. Ibid.

42. Ibid.

43. Norton A. Kaplan and Nicholas deB. Katzenbach, *The Political Foundation of International Law* (New York: Wiley, 1961), p. 188.

44. Interview with Senator McGovern, February 29, 1996.

45. Cong. Rec. S18406–8 (Daily ed., Aug. 6, 1964).

46. Ibid., 18408.

47. Ibid., 18409.

48. Ibid., 18422.

49. Cong. Rec. S18444 (Daily ed., Aug. 7, 1964).

50. From conversations with other staffers, heard by the author in early 1966.

51. Cong. Rec. S18446 (Daily ed., Aug. 7, 1964).

52. 1 Cranch 137 (1803).

53. Cong. Rec. S18459 (Daily ed., Aug. 7, 1964). The colloquy which allowed Senator Nelson the few minutes to introduce his amendment reads like a Marx Brothers comedy.

Mr. Nelson. Mr. President, will the Senator from Arkansas yield some time to the Senator from Wisconsin?

Mr. Fulbright. I shall be glad to do so. How much time does the Senator wish? Mr. President, how much time have we remaining?

The Presiding Officer. The Senator from Arkansas has nine minutes.

Mr. Fulbright. How much time would the Senator like?

Mr. Nelson. I do not understand the Chair's response. I thought thirty minutes were left.

The Presiding Officer. Under the unanimous-consent agreement, there is a time limitation. The Senator from Oregon has twenty-three minutes, and the Senator from Arkansas nine minutes.

Mr. Morse. Mr. President, I should like all that extra time, but I want to be fair. I do not have that much time. I would be glad to use it, but I want to be fair. The time started running at 10 o'clock. I finished at seven minutes to eleven, I believe. I will take the time if the Senator from Arkansas doesn't want it.

Mr. Nelson. I have an amendment to suggest. If the Senator from Arkansas accepted it, I would vote for the resolution. If it were not accepted, I might not. So whose time should I take?

Mr. Fulbright. I am perfectly willing to yield the Senator time. Mr. President, does the Chair have the time reversed?

The Presiding Officer. The Parliamentarian informs the Chair that the Senator from Arkansas has seven minutes left.

Mr. Nelson. Mr. President, not to take up all the time, would the Senator from Oregon yield me five minutes?

Mr. Morse. Mr. President, I understand the Senator from Wisconsin has an amendment to offer which might make the Joint Resolution a little better, but still unacceptable so far as I am concerned. Mr. President, how much time have I?

The Presiding Officer. Twenty-three minutes.

Mr. Morse. For the good of the cause, I will yield five minutes to the Senator from Wisconsin.

The Presiding Officer. The Senator from Wisconsin is recognized for five minutes.

54. Interview with Senator Gaylord Nelson, May 2, 1996.

55. The language of the Nelson amendment is cited in the Prologue.

56. Cong. Rec. S18459 (Daily ed., Aug. 7, 1964).

57. 84 Stat, 2053 section 12, (1971). The actual language of the repeal read: The Joint Resolution entitled "Joint Resolution to promote maintenance of international peace and security in Southeast Asia," approved August 10, 1964 (78 Stat. 384; Public Law 88–408), is terminated effective upon the day that the second session of the Ninety-first Congress is last adjourned.

58. As discussed in the Introduction concerning Fulbright's position on Cuba and Roosevelt's policies.

59. Randall B. Woods, *Fulbright, A Biography* (Cambridge: Cambridge University Press, 1995) p. 366.

60. See Reston's column in the *New York Times*, February 14, 1965, discussed in the Prologue.

61. Gilbert C. Fite, *Richard B. Russell, Senator from Georgia* (Chapel Hill: University of North Carolina Press, 1991), p. 338.

62. Ibid., p. 367.

63. Senator Sparkman had been Adlai Stevenson's running mate in 1952.

64. Randal B. Woods, *Fulbright, A Biography* (Cambridge: Cambridge University Press, 1995), p. 374.

65. Ibid., pp. 374–75.

3

WAS THERE AN AMERICAN POLICY IN VIETNAM?

"No more of this coup shit."
> —President Johnson to his staff in reference to
> the stability of South Vietnamese democracy.[1]

In short, the answer to the question: Was there an American policy in Vietnam at the time of the Gulf of Tonkin incident is yes; however, by year's end, no—a failure that led to the ultimate disastrous course of the war; with North Vietnam's total victory against the most powerful nation on earth. And the role of the U.S. Senate had the major impact on the question of the American policy that led to such a disaster.

Transcripts of presidential phone calls to Robert McNamara and McGeorge Bundy, recently released, reveal a perplexed president asking his Defense Secretary and National Security Advisor time and again for simple explanations of what was going on in the war.[2]

In one discussion, McNamara told the President, "There's just a lot of misunderstanding on it [Vietnam] in the country." LBJ asked, "Now what are we going to do? ... What is a one sentence statement of what our policy is out there?"[3]

It seems clear that Lyndon Johnson was thoroughly perplexed by what he recognized to be a complex issue, despite his simplistic public pronouncements about saving Vietnamese freedom. From his questioning of McNamara, one could conclude that McNamara was the President and LBJ a mere bewildered ordinary citizen.

The President further pressed McNamara, "I want you to dictate to me a memorandum—a couple of pages . . . so I can read it and study it and commit it to memory . . . on the situation in Vietnam."[4]

In fact, in a call to one of the National Security Advisors, Walt Rostow, on March 4, 1964, Johnson asked if Rostow had told *Washington Post* correspondent Chalmers Roberts that a presidential speech a few days before meant "an offensive in North Vietnam" was on the horizon. Rostow replied that he spoke to reporters of the administration's position to "hold Southeast Asia." Johnson replied, "Number one, I wouldn't talk to them [the press] at all, number two, the President doesn't know the position of the administration, so you can't know it."[5]

Despite presidential doubts and reluctance, which continued for some time, the real place to begin an analysis of U.S. policy during the Johnson years is with a speech delivered by Secretary McNamara on March 26, 1964, at the Forrestal Memorial Awards dinner in Washington. He began by stating . . .

My purpose this evening is three-fold. After recalling some facts about Vietnam and its history, I want:

- First, to explain our stake and objectives in South Vietnam;

- Second, to review for you the current situation there as General [Maxwell] Taylor and I found it on our recent trip;

- And finally, to outline in broad terms the plans which have been worked out with General [Nguyen] Khanh for achieving our mutual objectives in South Vietnam.

A simplistic explanation, which carries some truth, is that the stand against Communism in Vietnam was an extension of the anticommunism of the Cold War which also produced the Korean War, though McNamara's points were more subtle. This was not to be considered a continuation of the post-World War II concept of the United States as world policeman. In the second part of the speech Secretary McNamara listed three U.S. objectives. First, that South Vietnam is a "member of the Free World family" no matter how corrupt and how far from democracy it might be, years after President Eisenhower declared his extension of aid to the South Vietnamese to be based upon establishment of a corruption free democratic government.[6]

The second point McNamara cites is the strategic value of Vietnam to the defense of the United States, a version of the domino theory. Ironically, Johnson himself didn't take the domino theory seriously at all. His major concern was what the domestic political effect would be in case of a defeat.[7] More than thirty years later, in a news conference held in Hanoi by former Vietnamese and U.S. officials, Secretary McNamara conceded that the danger of the domino theory had been overstated. "Did we exaggerate the danger? I think so," Secretary McNamara said. "It is less and less likely to me that the Vietnamese would have permitted a unified independent Vietnam to be used as a Chinese base or a Russian base for extension of Chinese or Soviet hegemony across Asia. And yet, that's what we feared at the time."[8]

The third point was most critical, because it set the true basis for what was, at the outset, American policy. Citing a 1961 speech by Chairman Nikita Khrushchev, McNamara termed it "one of the most important speeches on Communist strategy in recent decades." Khrushchev's speech was an endorsement of so-called "wars of liberation." "World wars" he declared to be too dangerous, but referring to Vietnam, according to Secretary McNamara, Khrushchev said, "It is a sacred war." McNamara went on to find support for Khrushchev's strategy in the writings of Lenin and Mao. China is cited as supporting such wars with greater vigor than even the Soviet Union. With this reasoning, McNamara concluded the United States would "support the Government of South Vietnam in carrying out its anti-insurgency plan."

The most amazing part of the speech is on page 6 of the Department of Defense (DOD) Press Release in which the need and ability to suppress wars of liberation was, according to McNamara, proven by the defeat of insurgents in Malaya and the Philippines. How an intelligent man could equate these cases is astounding. In the Philippines, the populace clearly supported the government. So, too, in Malaya. The situations were wholly different than the Viet Cong insurgency, where a large percentage of the local populace opposed the government as a corrupt tyranny. Dean Rusk would constantly compare the Vietnam war to the Greek civil war, which the communists lost.[9] This, too, was a foolish analogy from which the Secretary of State never wavered. Indeed, one may safely conclude that Rusk's feet were firmly planted in the 1940s, never to move again.

Herein lies the basic American policy. Deal with the war of liberation, but do not get pulled into a major military action. Provoke a series of incidents, which will ultimately cause the North Vietnamese to react with hostility. Then clobber them, and the fear of confrontation with the most powerful nation on earth will cause them to tuck tail and back off with no real U.S. involvement or risk. And it seems as if the administration had no alternative fall-back position. So when the North Vietnamese did not cooperate with this show of force, the United States was left without a long-range policy and by the beginning of 1965 began to drift and react to events day by day, as South Vietnam's situation worsened day by day.

As early as March 1964, the time of McNamara's speech, he testified at closed hearings before the House Armed Services Committee, in testimony subsequently made public:

> *Mr. (Clarance) Long (D.-Md.).* If the Vietnamese war goes very badly, do you contemplate another Korean war from our point of view; our pouring in hundreds of thousands of troops?
>
> *Secretary McNamara.* No, sir.
>
> *Mr. Long.* You mentioned before that this is an area we must hold at all costs?
>
> *Secretary McNamara.* I don't believe that pouring in hundreds of thousands of troops is the solution to the problem in Vietnam.[10]

Johnson himself, from the time William Westmoreland asked for ground troops, began to fear another Korean war. Speaking to Bundy, the President's strained tone revealed his anxiety. "What alternative do we have then? We're not going to send our *troops* in there, are we?"[11] Mike Mansfield and J. William Fulbright had confronted him on that ground and Senator Richard Russell was said to be very concerned.[12]

Was the Secretary dissembling? I don't think so. Rather, I believe the administration truly did not know what the next step would be. The comparison of the Vietnamese civil war to the Philippine and Malaysian situations reveals, I believe, seriously flawed judgment. And it was that judgment together with Bundy's that formulated and carried on the Vietnam war.

Why did McNamara and Bundy exercise such great influence over Johnson, whose instincts were to avoid involvement in a Southeast Asia land war? Senator George McGovern is positive that the Great Society was Johnson's goal. He wanted to remake the face of American society, and to go down as the greatest President in history.[13] But other pressures were forcing him to make decisions he didn't want to make. Under Secretary of State George Ball, the only high ranking administration official to consistently express his opposition to the war to Johnson, summed up his judgment as to why Johnson fell into the trap he himself so desperately sought to avoid. Ball wrote in later years that one element that reinforced Johnson's failure to face reality in Vietnam was his sense of educational inferiority. He was overly impressed by the academic credentials of the men he had inherited from a particularly glamorous administration—at times expressing his sense of inferiority with, it seemed to Ball, a kind of silent, scornful envy, "G-ddamit, I made it without their advantages and now they're all working for me!" "No head of state," LBJ said, "ever had such a galaxy of talent. Dean Rusk, well, he was a Rhodes Scholar, a professor, then head of the Rockefeller Foundation. Bob McNamara was a professor at Harvard [he had been, in fact, an instructor at the Harvard Business School], then he ran the Ford Motor Company. Mac Bundy, here, is my in-house Ph.D. He was Dean up at Harvard." Ball said of the President, "Lyndon Johnson understood America but little of foreign countries or their history. He knew about the poor and the needy and the politics of farms and cities, but not about revolution in the Asian rice paddies. Had the war not occurred, he could have been a great President; instead, he must remain an ambiguous and compromised figure."[14]

Perhaps these, too, were factors that prevented LBJ from following Eisenhower's example of deflecting interventionist advice and following his own sound instincts to keep out.[15]

As Johnson leaned more and more toward McNamara and Bundy, with no senator in favor of their extreme position, pressures on him mounted.

Senator Lyndon Johnson opposed intervention in French Indo China in 1954. That opposition was not based upon inner conviction or deep understanding of the impossibility of success. Rather, the minority leader took the position of Senator Richard Russell, his mentor and advisor.[16]

Army Chief of Staff General Harold Johnson told LBJ at that same time that ultimate victory might require 500,000 U.S. troops for five years.[17] The numbers of troops for a planned escalation, while the President pledged to the nation not to commit ground troops, was awesome. General Johnson's words remind us of 1954, when General Matthew Ridgway said success on the ground in Vietnam would take between 500,000 and 1,000,000 troops.[18]

Senator Nelson recalls a February 1965 White House briefing at which a commitment of 75,000 troops was mentioned. Senator Nelson told me, "I didn't have a ride home but Hubert Humphrey, who was vice president, lived near me so I bummed a ride with him. I said Hubert, my G-d, if we send some ground troops in Vietnam, we will get into a hell of a big war, there's just no question about it. Well, with a note of amazement in his voice, he said that, look, there are people, you wouldn't believe it, there are people in the Pentagon and the State Department who want to send in 300,000 troops, exact quote, the President will never get sucked into that, and that was Hubert's belief."[19]

What does seem to emerge clearly is that after the retaliatory raids that followed the provocations in the Gulf of Tonkin there was no coherent American policy.[20]

Even after the July 1965 commitment of the original 75,000 troops, clandestine plans for further escalation were being formulated.[21]

Although the public was unaware of this planning, LBJ was briefing senators in groups of twenty-five or so.[22] The President was torn by indecision and doubts that did not seem to afflict his top advisors. By

January 1965, McNamara was the strongest hawk among Johnson's civilian advisors. Their advice and assurances served to calm the President's anxiety but led to further plans for escalation.[23]

At this time, George Ball was predicting a commitment of 500,000 troops, even before any ground forces had been officially authorized.[24] The president heard him out. Back in the fall of 1963, General Taylor had recommended to President John F. Kennedy the commitment of an additional 8,000 military advisors. Ball told Kennedy that the end result would be a wartime commitment of 300,000 within five years. (Actually, it reached over 500,000 in a bit more than five years.) Ball relates that President Kennedy laughed and said, "George, you're crazier than hell."[25]

Ironically, McNamara, in his memoirs, with a perspective of over thirty years, has written:

> But today I feel differently. Having reviewed the record in detail, and with the advantage of hindsight, I think it highly probable that, had President Kennedy lived, he would have pulled us out of Vietnam. He would have concluded that the South Vietnamese were incapable of defending themselves, and that Saigon's grave political weaknesses made it unwise to try to offset the limitations of South Vietnamese forces by sending U.S. combat troops on a large scale. I think he would have come to that conclusion even if he reasoned, as I believe he would have, that South Vietnam and, ultimately, Southeast Asia would then be lost to Communism. He would have viewed that loss as more costly than we see it now. But he would have accepted that cost because he would have sensed that the conditions he had laid down—i.e., it was a South Vietnamese war, that it could only be won by them, and to win it they needed a sound political base—could not be met. Kennedy would have agreed that withdrawal would cause a fall of the "dominoes" but that staying in would ultimately lead to the same result, while exacting a terrible price in blood.
>
> Early in his administration, President Kennedy asked his cabinet officials and members of the National Security Council to read Barbara Tuchman's book *The Guns of August*. He said it graphically portrayed how Europe's leaders had bungled into the debacle of World War I. And he emphasized: "I don't ever want to be in that position." Kennedy told us after we had done our reading, "We are not going to bungle into war."[26]

McNamara continues his analysis of President Kennedy's approach to setting policy and how he draws his conclusion that the president would not have conducted his policy as Johnson subsequently did. This analysis is particularly worthy of attention, coming from JFK's Secretary of Defense who was present at all the crises of 1961–1963.

> Throughout his presidency, Kennedy seemed to keep that lesson in mind. During the Bay of Pigs crisis in April 1961, against intense pressure from the CIA and the military chiefs, he kept to his conviction—as he had made explicitly clear to the Cuban exiles beforehand—that under no conditions would the United States intervene with military force to support the invasion. He held to this position even when it became evident that without that support the invasion would fail, as it did.
>
> I saw the same wisdom during the tense days of the Cuban Missile Crisis. By Saturday, October 27, 1962—the height of the crisis—the majority of the president's military and civilian advisers were prepared to recommend that if Khrushchev did not remove the Soviet missiles from Cuba (which he agreed to the following day) the United States should attack the island. But Kennedy repeatedly made the point that Saturday—both in Executive Committee sessions and later, in a small meeting with Bobby, Dean, Mac, and me—that the United States must make every effort to avoid the risk of an unpredictable war. He appeared willing, if necessary, to trade the obsolete American Jupiter missiles in Turkey for the Soviet missiles in Cuba in order to avert this risk. He knew such an action was strongly opposed by the Turks, by NATO, and by most senior U.S. State and Defense Department officials. But he was prepared to take that stand to keep us out of war.
>
> So I conclude that John Kennedy would have eventually gotten out of Vietnam rather than move more deeply in. I express this judgment now because, in light of it, I must explain how and why we—including Lyndon Johnson—who continued in policy-making roles after President Kennedy's death made the decision leading to the eventual deployment to Vietnam of half a million U.S. combat troops. Why did we do what we did, and what lessons can be learned from our actions?[27]

By November, McNamara was Johnson's leading hawk. In a November 8 memo to the President, the Secretary of Defense said that he, Under Secretary Rosewell Gilpatrick, and the Joint Chiefs of Staff thought that South Vietnam would fall without U.S. combat troops, which would not have to exceed six divisions, or 205,000 men.[28] This came a month after the President declared in the Akron campaign speech that American boys would not be sent to fight an Asian boys' war.

Under Secretary Ball maintained his opposition to McNamara's desired policy. President Johnson claimed to be carrying out President Kennedy's policies. Secretary McNamara now says this was not true. The difference is I believe that, under President Kennedy, McNamara was the administrator of the Department of Defense. Under LBJ, his role expanded to top advisor and formulator of policy. In short, therein lies the tragedy of the Vietnam War—the Secretary of Defense was extremely bright, but was not wise.

Secretary of the Navy Paul Nitze stated that only troops could turn the tide, but that to fail would be "to acknowledge that we couldn't beat the VC [and] the shape of the world will change."[29]

At the same time, the President was receiving different advice from respected former government officials. Just before the troop commitment decision became final by LBJ, Clark Clifford told him that George Ball's memorandum made a whole lot more sense than what McNamara, Bundy, and Rusk were saying. Johnson's aide, Jack Valenti, kept notes of what Clifford said. "Don't believe we can win in SVN. If we send in 100,000 more the NVN will meet us. If the NVN run out of men, the Chinese will send in volunteers. Russia and China don't intend for us to win the war. If we lose 50,000-plus, it will ruin us. Five years, billions of dollars, 50,000 men, it is not for us."

Throughout this post-election period there doesn't seem to be any strong force emanating from the Senate to urge caution and prudence by President Johnson. Yet, in fact, several of his oldest friends and mentors were arguing vehemently, in private, against escalation. Johnson succumbed to the pressure of the "Harvards."

In July 1965, LBJ was still receiving idiotic advice from Ambassador Henry Cabot Lodge that backing out of Vietnam would be "worse than a victory for the Kaiser or Hitler in the two world wars."[30] It is doubtful that LBJ gave any credence to such foolishness. Discussing Vietnam with Senator Russell, President Johnson said, "Now one of our big problems, Dick, the biggest between us—and I don't want this repeated to anybody—is Lodge. He ain't worth a damn."[31] But LBJ was deeply disturbed by the views of his old friend Senator Mansfield, Senate Majority Leader, who argued in a meeting with the president that the only pledge the United States had made was to assist the government of South Vietnam. But now there was no legitimate government to assist. Mansfield argued to get out on those grounds. This is the argument Westmoreland presented to Johnson.[32]

SENATOR RICHARD B. RUSSELL

There was one person, I believe, who might have been able to change President Johnson's policies, and who was consistently opposed to U.S.

intervention in Vietnam dating from the 1954 crisis under President Eisenhower,[33] and that was Senator Russell. Just as Senator Fulbright was the main figure in passage of the Gulf of Tonkin Resolution, Senator Russell was the key senator in allowing subsequent escalation and support of the war.

Senator Russell, in 1964 and until his death in 1971 chairman of the Senate Armed Services Committee, was the greatest enigma in the Senate. He publicly supported each step in the escalation, floor-managed each military appropriation bill, yet privately was as much a dove as Wayne Morse. I do not believe Russell's opposition to intervention was based on the same moralistic basis as that of the true dissidents such as Morse, Gruening, Nelson, McGovern, and Church. Even if his reasoning was merely strategic, he was the one with the prestige and influence to move Johnson from his reluctant belligerency.

Senator Russell entered the Senate at the time of Franklin Roosevelt's first term. He always supported the national Democratic ticket, even during the Dixiecrat revolt in 1948. At first he was an enthusiastic New Dealer, but he grew conservative with the years. Yet he supported selective liberal Democratic legislation, sponsored by the Roosevelt and Truman and Kennedy administrations, for relief of agriculture and projects such as rural electrification. The burden he carried, which prevented him from becoming a true national leader within the party, was his unyielding, obstinate hostility to civil rights and continued leadership of the congressional segregationists.[34]

In 1952, Russell was a serious candidate for the Democratic presidential nomination. On the first ballot in Chicago, Senator Estes Kefauver led with 340 votes, Adlai Stevenson followed with 273, and Russell trailed a close third with 268.[35] But his support was almost entirely in the South and he never rose higher. President Truman told Russell that if he'd come from Indiana or Missouri, "You would be elected president hands down."[36] He masterfully defused the potentially volatile constitutional crisis after the dismissal of General Douglas MacArthur by Harry Truman in 1951. Closed hearings, with extended questioning, led Congress to see that Truman's position was correct under the constitutional system. All this was the craft of Richard Russell.[37]

Russell was one of the two members of the Warren Commission who initially refused to sign the report because he said it was not supported by the evidence. How he was pressured into signing is the subject for another work. But the point is that he maintained his independence even in the face of powerful and influential opposition.

As early as the time of his 1954 opposition to intervention in Vietnam, the puzzle of who was Richard Russell emerged. He had already demonstrated his tenacity in opposing intervention in the April 1954 White House meeting.[38]

Later, when President Eisenhower had decided against intervention, he nevertheless decided to send the 200 advisors, and he sent then Under Secretary of State Thruston Morton to inform Senator Russell as a courtesy. Russell replied that it would not stay at 200. It would rise to 20,000 and perhaps one day to 200,000. "I think this is the greatest mistake this country's ever made," Russell said, "I could not be more opposed to it." But he then told Morton to tell President Eisenhower, "if he does it I will never raise my voice."[39]

The first public awareness of Russell's opposition to the Vietnam war during the Johnson years came through a *New York Times* piece on November 27, 1964. After a visit to Johnson, he said the United States must help South Vietnam or get out. The South Vietnamese will not help themselves and our involvement was a "big mistake."[40] In the *Times* of December 31, Russell is quoted as having told a reporter that the United States "made a terrible mistake getting involved in Vietnam. I don't know just how we can get out now, but the time is about at hand when we must re-evaluate our position."[41]

Russell, in a conversation with President Johnson, caused LBJ to express his own reservations in a way he would not likely have revealed to anyone else. Russell said, "It's the damn worst mess I ever saw and I don't like to brag. I never have been right many times in my life. But I knew that we were going to get into this sort of mess when we went in there. And I don't see how we're ever going to get out of it without fighting a major war with China and all of them down there in those rice paddies and jungles." The President replied, "That's the way I've been feeling for six months. How important is it [Vietnam] to us?" Russell replied, "It isn't important a damn bit, with all these new missile systems."[42]

From the very beginning, Russell gave LBJ his true opinions and advice. Shortly after Johnson took office, Senator Russell came out from a meeting with the new president and told Juanita Roberts, the President's private secretary, "Missy, it's a mistake. He ought not to keep them. It's a mistake and I've told him so."[43] The reference was to McNamara and Mac Bundy, whom Johnson was praising. Russell considered McNamara a man whose "enthusiasm clouds his judgement in the area of international relations." He also was quoted as regretfully concluding that McNamara "exercised some hypnotic influence" over LBJ.[44] On yet another occasion, Russell remarked to Johnson, "I'm not too sure he [McNamara] understands the history and background of those people out there as fully as he should." LBJ replied, somewhat bitterly, "I spend all my days with Rusk and McNamara and Bundy and [Averell] Harriman. . . . They're kind of like MacArthur in Korea. They don't believe the Chinese communists will come into this thing, but they don't know." "I don't think the people of the country know much about Vietnam and I think they care a hell of a lot less," President Johnson concluded.[45]

Senator Russell did not waver from the position he took in 1954. Unlike Fulbright, whose views ranged from LBJ's leading spokesman and apologist in the Senate to a main critic, Senator Russell had clear judgment throughout the prewar period and during the war. During the Kennedy years, when some pushed for a greater American military role in Vietnam, Russell warned the president in a phone call, "I hope you will take a long, hard look before you commit anybody over there. . . . It would be a festering sore. We'd be still sitting there three or four years from now."[46]

During the holiday season in December 1964, Senator Russell called a journalist friend from his home in Georgia and said to him . . .

> I see you have just been in Vietnam, and I would like to get your impression of the situation out there. But first, let me tell you my impression which I am inclined to give my friend, who called me from the [LBJ] ranch this afternoon. He said they have just blown up the Brinks officers' quarters in Saigon, and on top of that the South Vietnamese government seems to be trying to declare Max Taylor persona non grata. I am inclined to tell the president when I call him back that if I were president I would sail the Seventh Fleet up the Saigon River, load those 23,000 Americans aboard and bring them home.[47]

There is little record of LBJ-Russell correspondence concerning the war, but they spoke about it constantly.

In a letter to a constituent in June 1965, Russell made it clear that his views on U.S. intervention in Southeast Asia had not changed through the years: "I have never seen where Vietnam has strategic, tactical, or economic value, and in addition to the billions we are spending there now, we lost three billion down the drain supporting the French in Dien Bien Phu."[48]

Despite the consistency of Russell's private opposition to the war, and the rising intensity of that opposition, he never wavered from public support of the president. Just as he had told Thruston Morton in 1957 to tell President Eisenhower not to send advisors, but if Ike did that he would remain silent,[49] so too did he remain steadfast in public support of LBJ. That silence, however, fell into place after the shooting began. In May 1964, Russell did state his views publicly. In opposing the sending of ground troops to Vietnam, Russell wrote, "I would rather pull out entirely with whatever loss of face this might bring, for I am convinced that we would be bogged down in the jungle fighting Chinese in their kind of war for the next 25 years."[50]

That same month, when Senator Morse tried to learn the administration's plans for sending troops to Vietnam, Russell said on the Senate floor, "I could not see any strategic tactical or economic value in that

area. In the day of long range planes and missiles that area has no significant value as a base for military operations."[51]

Senator Morse, recognizing the significance of Russell's remarks, said
that they were "the most important statement that has been made to
date by anyone in the country on the folly of the South Vietnam operations."[52] Privately, Russell was even more critical about the effectiveness
of the bombing. He exclaimed to LBJ, "Bomb the North and kill old men,
women, and children?" Johnson answered, "No, they say pick out an oil
plant . . . or something like that." Russell replied, "Oh, hell, that ain't
worth a hoot. That's just impossible." Johnson agreed, "McNamara said
yesterday that in Korea that LeMay and all of 'em were gong to stop all
those tanks. There's ninety come through. They turned all the Air Force
loose on them. They got one. Eighty-nine come on through."[53]

So, incredible as it seems, Russell, thought to be the arch hawk, and
Morse, the dove, at least this one time were in total agreement.

Senator Nelson related that there was a small senator's dining room
which would seat only six or eight persons. He used to have lunch there
together with Senators Russell, Allen Ellender, and some of the other
old-time Southerners, enjoying hearing their stories. Some of them had
come to the Senate during Roosevelt's first term in 1933. Senator Nelson
told the author that Russell consistently floor-managed the supplemental
appropriations, never uttering a word in public of his private feeling
which he made clear to President Johnson. Nelson said, "I talked with
Dick Russell and in the first place he had an enormous respect for the
right of the President to manage foreign policy. Now obviously he knew
that only Congress could declare war, but he had a respect for that and
he was Chairman of the Armed Services Committee and what he was
thinking was—but I don't think he was right—well, if I don't come up
with that supplemental, I am leaving our boys stranded, and I don't want
to be in that position, that's what he told me in lunchtime conversation."[54]

After searching all available sources, it emerges that the only explanation for why Russell's public silence came after the shooting began
was based on two factors. First, he had a misguided sense of what was
respect for the president, and of the need to support the flag once committed. More important was his total lack of understanding of congressional responsibility in exercising power over the executive under Article
I, §8, of the Constitution.

Upon further reflection, one is forced to reach the conclusion that this
man of integrity and honesty, who had it within his power to shorten
or to end the war entirely, refused to exercise his enormous influence
because of those misguided errors in judgment. Knowing that the war
was pointless and doomed to failure, Senator Russell, together with Mc-
Namara, whose doubts emerged in 1966, nevertheless allowed it to con-

tinue, and for tens of thousands of Americans as well as an incalculable number of Vietnamese to die—for no purpose other than that the flag was committed.

Toward the end of 1964, the lack of long-term U.S. policy became apparent. Russell had urged that the bungling Ambassador Lodge be replaced by General Maxwell Taylor. It appears that Johnson reluctantly agreed to the first steps of escalation over Thanksgiving, 1964. Ambassador Maxwell Taylor, in an incredible cable, said that "If the government falters and gives good reason to believe that it will never attain the desired level of performance, I would favor going against the North anyway. The purpose of such an attack would be to give pulmotor treatment for a government in extremis and to make sure that the DRV does not get off unscathed in any final settlement."[55] Yet until the end Taylor opposed use of ground troops, and he was referring only to air strikes.

President Johnson's level of enthusiasm for the planned escalation was far less. He told a visitor that all that the Joint Chiefs did was come in every morning and tell him, "Bomb, bomb, bomb," and come back every afternoon and repeat, "Bomb, bomb, bomb."[56]

Bundy told the President he was going to lunch with Joe Alsop, the hawkish columnist. Johnson snapped sarcastically, "I'd ask him what his program is. I'd ask him if he wants to send people in there and start another Korea."[57]

According to Charles Roberts of *Newsweek*, and later reported by Tom Wicker, the bombing targets were selected by October 1964,[58] that is, before the election, while Johnson was campaigning on a promise of no wider war. The targets were selected on a contingency basis. Admiral U.S. Grant Sharp had disclosed the two contingency plans for bombing North Vietnam were Flaming Dart and Rolling Thunder. Flaming Dart raids were to be in response to specific provocation, while Rolling Thunder was to be an ongoing campaign.[59]

The senatorial briefings by Johnson, described by Senator Nelson, were the first steps by the President to twist the meaning of the Tonkin Gulf Resolution into something far beyond its stated purpose and its meaning as defined by Fulbright. The resolution was converted into a grant of authority to escalate the war.

NOTES

1. David Halberstam, *The Best and the Brightest* (New York: Random House, 1969), p. 352. This occurred in early 1964.

2. Walter Pincus, *Washington Post*, p. A40, October 12, 1996.

3. Michael Beschloss, *Taking Charge: The Johnson White House Tapes, 1963–64* (New York: Simon and Schuster, 1997), p. 293.

4. Ibid., p. 257.

5. Ibid.

6. Dwight Eisenhower, *Public Papers of the Presidents* (Washington, D.C.: Government Printing Office, 1954), No. 3 and 6.

7. I. F. Stone, *A Time of Torment* (New York: Random House, 1967), p. 193.

8. *Baltimore Sun*, June 24, 1997, p. 7A

9. Lloyd Gardner, *Pay Any Price* (Chicago: Ivan R. Dee Publishers, 1995), p. 173.

10. Stone, *A Time of Torment*, p. 193.

11. Beschloss, *Taking Charge*, p. 263.

12. Gardner, *Pay Any Price*, pp. 220–21.

13. Interview with Senator George McGovern, February 29, 1996.

14. George Ball, *The Past Has Another Pattern* (New York: W. W. Norton, 1982), p. 426.

15. As discussed in this chapter.

16. Gilbert C. Fite, *Richard B. Russell, Senator from Georgia* (Chapel Hill: The University of North Carolina Press, 1991), p. 358.

17. Gardner, *Pay Any Price*, p. 220.

18. As discussed in Chapter 1.

19. Interview with Senator Gaylord Nelson, May 2, 1996.

20. This note is the text of a report provided Senator Nelson in July 1965, which includes projections made during early July when there were no official American combatants in Vietnam.

Legislative Reference Service   July 16, 1965
TO: The Honorable Gaylord Nelson

FROM: Foreign Affairs Division

SUBJECT: Estimates of U.S. troops needed in Vietnam, and when U.S. dropped non-combat terminology

According to Howard Margolis (*Washington Post*, July 15, 1965) the presently announced commitment of U.S. military personnel will bring the total to 80,000. He estimates that a commitment of 150,000 is possible, based on the service requests for reservists.

Fred S. Hoffman of the Associated Press says that the Joint Chiefs of Staff have unanimously recommended that U.S. manpower be boosted to 179,000 by the end of the year (*Washington Post*, July 16, 1965). This apparently was denied by Secretary McNamara.

Stewart Alsop (*Saturday Evening Post*, July 17, 1965) said that Secretary McNamara has privately talked of the need for 300,000 Americans, and that Korea scale war may emerge (Article reprinted in *Congressional Record*, July 12, 1965, p. 15873).

After the Vietcong attack on the Bien Hoa airbase of November 1, 1964, the U.S. buildup continued and American spokesmen were still officially referring to the new personnel as needed to bolster advisory cadres and not reflecting any change in policy (John Maffre, *Washington Post*, December 6, 1965).

In February 1965, it was reported that the United States was considering sending a small number of troops (apparently the word used by the unidentified U.S. source) to Vietnam, particularly to protect American installations. The largest previous increase took place in Summer 1964 when "adviser" personnel were increased from the 16,000 mark (John W. Finney, *New York Times*, February 13, 1965).

John G. Norris reported on February 17, 1965 that U.S. official spokesmen had dropped the fiction that U.S. personnel were non-combatants (*Washington Post*, February 17, 1965, article enclosed).

The adviser function, however, has not ceased to exist and the term is still used to refer to Americans attached to South Vietnamese Army and Navy units.

Cedric W. Tarr, Jr.
Analyst in National Defense

21. Ibid.

22. Interview with Senator Gaylord Nelson, May 2, 1996.

23. David M. Barrett, *Uncertain Warrior* (Lawrence: University of Kansas Press, 1993), p. 29.

24. Halberstam, *The Best and the Brightest*, pp. 173–74.

25. Ibid., p. 173.

26. Robert McNamara, *In Retrospect* (New York: Random House, 1995), p. 96.

27. Ibid., p. 97.

28. Gardner, *Pay Any Price*, p. 246.

29. Ibid., p. 149.

30. Ibid., p. 250.

31. Beschloss, *Taking Charge*, p. 250.

32. Ibid.

33. As discussed in Chapter 1.

34. For the background of Senator Russell's career and political positions, see Gilbert C. Fite, *Richard B. Russell, Senator from Georgia* (Chapel Hill: University of North Carolina Press, 1991).

35. Ibid., p. 295.

36. Ibid., p. 290.

37. Ibid., pp. 259–64.

38. As discussed in this chapter.

39. Halberstam, *The Best and the Brightest*, p. 146.

40. *New York Times*, November 27, 1964, p. 17:1.

41. *New York Times*, December 31, 1964, p. 4:3.

42. Beschloss, *Taking Charge*, p. 363.

43. Gardner, *Pay Any Price*, p. 93.

44. Barrett, *Uncertain Warrior*, p. 25.

45. Beschloss, *Taking Charge*, pp. 363–64.

46. David Schoenbrum, *Vietnam. How We Got In, How to Get Out* (New York: Atheneum, 1968), p. 12.

47. Barrett, *Uncertain Warrior*, p. 34.

48. Russell archives, Georgia.

49. Halberstam, *The Best and the Brightest*, p. 146.

50. Fite, *Richard B. Russell*, p. 437.

51. Cong. Rec. S6629–30 (Daily ed., March 31, 1964).

52. Ibid.

53. Beschloss, *Taking Charge*, p. 369.

54. Interview with Senator Gaylord Nelson, May 2, 1996.

55. Gardner, *Pay Any Price*, p. 152.

56. Ibid.

57. Beschloss, *Taking Charge*, p. 262.

58. Gardner, *Pay Any Price*, p. 152.

59. Eugene Windchy, *Tonkin Gulf* at 320.

TOP: Holding a conference in the plane on September 12, 1964. From left Senator Richard Russell; Governor Carl Sanders (Georgia); Representative J. Russell Tuten; Senator Herman Talmadge; Edward McDermott, director of the Office of Emergency Planning; President Johnson and Anthony Celebreze, director of Health Education and Welfare. Photo courtesy of AP/World Wide Photos.

BOTTOM: McGeorge Bundy, right, shown in a January 31, 1966 photo with President Johnson, left, and press secretary Bill Moyers, center, a key adviser to President Johnson. Photo courtesy of AP/World Wide Photos.

TOP: Secretary of Defense Robert S. McNamara, left, with President Johnson. Photo courtesy of AP/World Wide Photos.

BOTTOM: George McGovern.

TOP: Senator Gaylord Nelson, left, with President John F. Kennedy.

BOTTOM: Senator Gaylord Nelson, left, with author Ezra Siff.

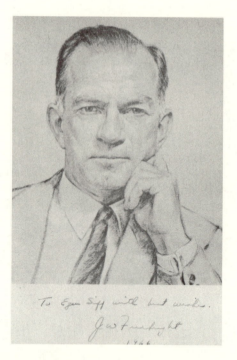

TOP: J. W. Fulbright.

BOTTOM: Senator Wayne Morse.

4

THE GATHERING STORM

Bomb, Bomb, Bomb. That's all you know. Well I want to know why
there's nothing else . . . you're not giving me any ideas and any so-
lutions for this damn little pissant country. . . . I want some answers.[1]
—President Johnson to General Johnson,
Army Chief of Staff, in March 1965.

During the period between passage of the Gulf of Tonkin Resolution in
August 1964 and the massive bombing of March 1965, Senator Frank
Church (D.-Idaho) became an important factor in opposition to the war.

Senator Church had a somewhat mixed record previously on Vietnam.
As early as June 23, 1964, six weeks before the Gulf of Tonkin events,
Senator Church anticipated the expansion of the war and opposed any
escalation. The basis for his opinion was the incompetence of the South
Vietnamese army and the presence of 25,000 highly motivated Viet Cong
insurgents. With what appeared to be a prescient look into the near future, Senator Church said:

Do we think that the bombing of North Vietnam will break the
spirit of the Government, and cause it to discontinue to aid and
abet the insurrection in the south? Why should we? The bombing
of North Korea never broke the spirit there. And we bombed

every house, bridge, and road until there was nothing left but rubble. Expanding the war is not getting out, Mr. President. It is getting further in.[2]

Anticipating that the extensive bombing would create a situation analogous to Korea played to Lyndon Johnson's greatest fear. Senator Church's remarks of June 23, 1964, were praised on the Senate floor by as diverse a group as Senators Wayne Morse, William Proxmire (D.-Wis.), Claiborne Pell (D.-R.I.), and future Vice-President Hubert Humphrey.[3]

Amazingly, Senator Church, who had shown such perception in his June remarks, said during the consideration of the Gulf of Tonkin Resolution on August 6, "The President is to be commended for the restraint as well as for the promptness and effectiveness of the American retaliation."[4] Nevertheless, Church concluded: "My misgivings have not been dissipated by the ominous events of the past few days. Rather they have been intensified. Because who can say these events are not the natural consequence of the hazards we have assumed by the policy we have adopted in this part of the world."[5]

So although maintaining his basic conviction that the entire thrust of our Southeast Asia policy was erroneous, Church still went on record as voting for the Gulf of Tonkin Resolution that put him in the same category as other early opponents to administration policy, such as Senators Gaylord Nelson, George McGovern, and Mike Mansfield, all of whom relied upon J. William Fulbright's disclaimers—the significant difference being that until well into 1965 Fulbright himself remained a true believer and leader in support of Johnson's policy. Church's remarks revealed a perception and anxiety that perhaps his vote was wrong: "Congress shares its responsibility for that policy. If we have not formulated it we have funded it from year to year with our votes. Who is there to say that we have not acquiesced in it through the years? . . . It is in this spirit that I approach the pending joint resolution. Under the circumstances we must unite behind the President."[6] Despite his vote for the Gulf of Tonkin Resolution, Senator McGovern told this author in 1996 that Senator Church was opposed to the war policy consistently, from the very beginning.[7]

Besides those senators who spoke out publicly in opposition to administration policy, there were also closet doves who felt behind the scene influence in committee would be more effective.

It was apparent that Senator Albert Gore (D.-Tenn.), father of the future vice-president, fully believed Robert McNamara's version of the Gulf of Tonkin incident, but he praised Senator Church's August 6 remarks as "candid and courageous."[8] Senator Gore explained his failure to have gone public with his privately held views:

Mr. Gore. The able Senator [Church] has lucidly put forward his reservations and doubts. Although I have not publicly voiced my doubts, as has the Senator from Idaho, nevertheless, it is the duty of a Senator to advise and consent. I have, in the executive sessions of the committee, expressed deep concern and I have raised critical questions as the Senator from Idaho will recall, about U.S. policy in Vietnam.

Perhaps I was remiss in not giving public expression to these views. But every Member of this body performs his duty as he sees it. It had been my view that I could perform best and most responsively in executive sessions of the committee.

Now, however, when U.S. forces have been attacked repeatedly upon the high seas, as I said immediately upon the convening of the Senate after the second attack, whatever doubts one may have entertained are water over the dam. Freedom of the seas must be preserved. Aggression against our forces must be repulsed.

I compliment the Senator and associate myself with almost all the sentiments he has expressed.

To go further back, I was one of those who did not think it wise for the United States to undertake this burden after the fall of Dienbienphu. That, too, is history. We must act today in light of facts today.

I join the Senator in the conclusion he reaches in support of the joint resolution. I join him, too, in confidence that President Johnson will act with prudence, caution, and wisdom, and with the courage necessary for the eventualities that may come.

Mr. Church. I thank the Senator very much for his remarks. I appreciate them more than I can say.[9]

Later, during the war, Senator Gore realized that Johnson was not acting with "prudence" and joined the active doves. Senator John Sherman Cooper, a moderate Republican from Kentucky, was another to express reservations about the government's policy but accepted Fulbright's assurances that the President would follow a prudent course.[10]

Those who ultimately took a public stand opposing U.S. policy in Vietnam differed as to the most effective way to terminate the war. Senator McGovern explained to me that he, Senator Church, and later Senator Fulbright, after his transfiguration to a dove, favored a systematic program of public education through speeches and extensive hearings. Senators Nelson, Morse, and Ernest Gruening believed the appropriation weapon should be used as well.[11] This would explain and attempt to

justify the votes cast in favor of military appropriations bills by opponents of government policy, while for years the only ones to vote "no"
were Morse, Nelson, and Gruening.

THE CHURCH SPEECH OF FEBRUARY 17, 1965

As part of the plan to educate and convince the public that government
policy was in error, Senator Church prepared several scholarly speeches
to be given in the Senate. The speeches were delivered against an increasingly ominous background. On February 7, the U.S. barracks at
Pleiku were attacked at night, with U.S. casualties. The *New York Times*
urged that President de Gaulle's offer to arrange negotiations be accepted. The United States refused. After the Rolling Thunder bombing
began, in a March 2, 1965 conversation in the Oval Office, President
Johnson told Senator McGovern with great intensity, referring to the
Pleiku attack, "they killed those boys while they were sleeping." Mc-
Govern replied, "That is the way war is, even General Washington
crossed the Delaware on Christmas Eve to carry out an attack." The
analogy did not please the President.[12]

On February 14, Reston's column in the *Times* appeared saying we
were in an undeclared and unexplained war. From the press of those
days one gets the impression that it was felt that the United States was
drifting into something terrible but would not or could not stop it. On
February 11, the Viet Cong hit the U.S. barracks at Qui Nhom. Unbe-
known to Congress or the public, the decision to go with the Rolling
Thunder bombing was taken on February 13. The original plan was for
one raid a week, later to be increased to ten to twelve a week by July
15.[13]

Church's main speech was delivered in the Senate on February 17,
1965. McNamara's March 1964 speech analyzed why we were in Vietnam. His prime reason was to stop the wars of liberation, Khruschev's
"holy wars." Senator Church, without reference to McNamara's position,
effectively refuted the premise of administration policy and the frame of
mind which led to McNamara's March 1964 speech.

> Why have we spread ourselves so thin? What compulsion draws
> us, ever deeper, into the internal affairs of so many countries in
> Africa and Asia, having so remote a connection with the vital
> interests of the United States?
> The answer, I think, stems from our intensely ideological view
> of the cold war. We have come to treat "communism," regard-
> less of what form it may take in any given country, as the enemy.
> We fancy ourselves as guardian of the "free" world, though
> most of it is not free, and never has been. We seek to immunize

this world against further Communist infection through massive injections of American aid, and, wherever necessary, through direct American intervention. Such a vast undertaking has at least two defects: First, it exceeds our national capability; second, among the newly emerging nations, where the specter of Western imperialism is dreaded more than communism, such a policy can be self-defeating. As a seasoned, friendly foreign diplomat recently put it. "The United States is getting involved in situations where no one—not even a nation of saints—would be welcome."

This is not to say that we should write off Africa or Asia. It is to say that a foreign policy of intervention, which was right for Western Europe, is apt to be wrong for those continents which have just thrown off European rule.

To begin with, the stakes in Europe were different. Had so rich an industrial prize as Western Europe ever fallen into Russian hands, the actual balance of power in the world would have shifted from us to the Soviet Union. We were obliged to regard the dividing line in Europe as though it were an American frontier, to commit our nuclear arsenal to its defense, and to station an army of American troops in West Germany as "tripwire" evidence of our determination to defend that country as though it were our own.[14]

Church's analysis is not necessarily of the different forms of communism, but of the vastly different circumstances when vital American interests are threatened and a strong argument for intervention made. This, incredibly, is what such supposedly intelligent men such as McNamara, McGeorge Bundy, and all the rest missed.

Senator Church continued to say that even if our presence in Vietnam was justified once, by February 17, 1965, the policy was bankrupt.

To the case against excessive American intervention in Africa and Asia, the State Department has a stock answer: The Communists will not let us quit. South Vietnam is pointed to as the proof of our dilemma. If we permit the Vietcong to overthrow the Saigon Government, then the gates are open, so the argument goes, to successful Communist subversion of all the other governments in southeast Asia.

But the hard fact is that there are limits to what we can do in helping any government surmount a Communist uprising. If the people themselves will not support the Government in power, we cannot save it. We can give arms, money, food, and supplies, but the outcome will depend, in the final analysis, upon the character of the Government helped, and the extent to which the people are willing to rally behind it.

The Saigon Government is losing its war not for lack of equipment, but for lack of internal cohesion. The Vietcong grow stronger, not because they are better supplied than Saigon, but because they are united in their will to fight. This spirit cannot be imported; it must come from within. It is nothing that we Americans can supply from our side of the Pacific. The weakness in South Vietnam emanates from Saigon itself, where we, as foreigners, are powerless to unite the spoiling factions. A family feud is never settled by outsiders. Only the Vietnamese themselves can furnish the solution.

As to the other governments in southeast Asia, they are not so many dominoes in a row. They differ from one another in popular support, and in capacity to resist Communist subversion. The Malayans, with British help, because of their own determined resistance to communism, successfully put down a long and bloody insurrection. Guerrilla wars—even when nourished from without—can be won by sitting governments but only in countries where shelter for the enemy is not furnished by the people themselves.[15]

Johnson himself was skeptical of the domino theory. Senators Morse and Gruening had, of course, in Senate speeches, argued the illogic of the domino theory consistently, while most public officials accepted it as dogma. Senator Church's speech provided the first detailed analysis by another senator that challenged the validity of the theory, which was one of the bases of U.S. policy in Vietnam, as stated in the McNamara speech of March 1964[16]—first that the administration's course of action was based upon false assumptions, and second that it was not effective.

President John Kennedy in his last public remarks on Vietnam in September 1963 in an interview with Walter Cronkite, seemed to both endorse the domino theory and reject its consequences at the same time.[17]

Even before the heavy bombing became official policy, Senator Church in his address again reiterated:

The systematic and sustained bombing of North Vietnam, unattended by any proffered recourse to the bargaining table, can only lead us into war. North Vietnam, lacking air and sea power, must answer on the ground. Her response, in the form of added military pressures against the south, Saigon can hardly be expected to withstand. As a consequence, the next step will be to send American land forces into battle, thus converting the struggle into an American war on the Asian mainland. That China will, sooner or later, enter such a war, I have no doubt.[18]

The clandestine planning for the land war was being carried out even as he spoke. His speech was one of the first challenges to the widely accepted, inviolate doctrine of the domino theory, a speech which foresaw the futility of the future bombing and the inevitable land war that would follow.

Senator Church's speech was followed by a colloquy, primarily with Senator McGovern. Church stated, again with justified foreboding, that without negotiations, ground war would escalate beyond control.[19] McGovern added that the administration policy was actually healing the latest splits in Communist parties and solidifying the movement.

> *Mr. McGovern.* Mr. President, the Senator has touched on one of the most fundamental questions in this whole crisis area. It would be the saddest of misfortunes if, at a time when the Communist world appears to be in disarray and the monolithic Communist bloc which once confronted us has been shattered, we were to provide through our actions the vehicle that united these very Communist governments. I can see that very thing happening in the event of an all-out war in Southeast Asia. It would cause our Communist rivals to close ranks as nothing else could. Beyond that we would have set back the cause of a detente of peaceful relationship of the kind that we hope has been developing between Red China and the Soviet Union.[20]

An intense debate followed the speech between Senator Church and Senator Gale McGee (D.-Wy.), an administration supporter. One can only wonder what would have happened if these discussions of diverse views had taken place before the Gulf of Tonkin Resolution enactment. McGee still believed in an aggressive communist system seeking *lebensraum* and the need to further contain communism in Vietnam.

> *Senator McGee.* Mr. President, those men have never gotten out of the notion that we will not see it through. They have the parallel of World War II. We went home much sooner then than this time. This time we have changed the parallel. We have learned the lesson of 1918. However, the fact remains that those men read American history. Of course, sometimes they read only what they want to read, but it is understandable that Asians still believe that we will grow tired and go away. When I say that, I need not remind the distinguished Senator from Idaho and the

Senator from South Dakota [Mr. McGovern], now occupying the Presiding Officer's chair, that even our friends in Europe entertain such misgivings. One of the almost regular concepts that worries them, that gives them unrest, is the fact that if the Americans do not go home in the first 10 years, they are sure to go home in the second 10 years.

I doubt that in the history of our time, at least, there will ever be a moment in the struggle when we will dare go home. I am afraid that times will compel us to man the ramparts, the frontiers of power politics all around the globe for the foreseeable future. They are confident that we will pack up our tents and leave. They want to find out whether this is the time. That is why they are sticking their fingers into Vietnam right now. I personally do not believe they intend this to be the ultimate showdown, but I think they are trying to take a reading on our intentions.

I repeat, given the Communist mind and given the mystery of what we read in the newspapers, and the debates on the floor of the Senate—and we often find it difficult to understand each other—it does not require much imagination to understand that some of the men in Hanoi may not be getting the message loud and clear from Washington. That is the basis of my concern.[21]

So Senator McGee, an intelligent, perceptive man, still clutched onto the need of a policy of containment of what he perceived as a monolithic communist movement. His views expressed that day were an accurate expression of those of McNamara, Bundy, and ultimately LBJ himself.

Ironically, former Ambassador George Kennan, author of the containment policy in the late 1940s for Europe, held the policy invalid when applied to Vietnam. At the later Foreign Relations Committee hearings in February 1968 Kennan said, "If we were not already involved as we are today in Vietnam, I know of no reason why we should be."[22]

An important reason for senators not to criticize administration policy was stated by Senator McGee when he said "some of the men in Hanoi may not be getting the message loud and clear."

Senator Nelson relates a story in a similar vein, that he, Senators McGovern, Ted Kennedy, and Edmund Muskie were briefed by General Maxwell Taylor. Nelson says that the reason was that they were saying things against U.S. policy. The senator added,

I don't know why Muskie was there because he was hawk all the way.

But in any event Taylor comes up and he's very attractive intellectually and personally, and he said I loved the speeches that you're making on the floor. They're very well, very high quality, but he said the trouble was that when the speeches are made and then they get into the government of North Vietnam, then they interpret that as the United States was soft on Vietnam to the world. Which would be understandable in the sense that if anybody did that over there they'd be shot. And so, after he said that I said, are you telling us that we should give up the right of free speech, free expression, just because some Communist leader doesn't understand what freedom is about?[23]

Nevertheless, even during the period of the Church-McGovern speeches and the tension caused by the attacks on U.S. troops, the doves of later years didn't push the issue. No one rationally believed a ground war with 500,000 troops was imminent. The administration denied any such intent. Perhaps most importantly, the Senate foreign policy leader, Senator Fulbright, was at this time still in full support of the President's position.

Comparisons of the administration critics to the appeasers of the 1930s also became part of the dialogue. Senator McGee said:

I hope it will not be interpreted wrongly if I were to suggest that the hope that may be expressed and is expressed daily in the press by some, that China really will not be up to anything very serious, reminds us of the speculation that went on about what Mr. Hitler might do, or what Mr. Mussolini might or might not do, in the time previous to World War II.[24]

And so the specter of China as a potential world conqueror was thrown into the picture. China, without a navy, without an industrial base, without steel production, could not be appeased by America abandoning South Vietnam.

Minority Leader Everett Dirksen used the smear tactic he had refined during the not so long before McCarthy era, when he called the Church speech a call "to run up the white flag."[25]

In later months, during a speech on Vietnam in the Senate, Dirksen referred to Senator Nelson as "comrade Nelson." This slur was made to an almost empty chamber, but I was present and told Nelson what Dirksen had said. Nelson confronted him privately, and Dirksen brushed it off as a misunderstanding. But as one of the few who were present, I can attest that the remark was one of Dirksen's patented smears.[26]

Johnson's reaction to Senator Church's speeches was harsh and hostile. Richard Goodwin has stated that the tragedy of LBJ's reaction was that Church possessed precisely what the policy makers lacked—historical perspective and the need for informed debate in a democracy.[27]

As a sidelight to the February 17 speech, Senators Church and Mc-
Govern were invited to the White House on the evening of February 18,
with their wives, for a reception, after which Johnson was to give a briefing on Vietnam. There, Johnson cornered Church for a long bitter lecture.
Senator Ralph Yarborough of Texas got the impression that LBJ was
"bawling out" Church. Church replied that what he was saying didn't
differ from the columns of Walter Lippmann. Johnson replied, "Well,
Frank, next time you need a dam in Idaho, go ask Walter Lippmann for
one."

Church was next at the White House on April 7, to be briefed with
other senators on Johnson's upcoming speech at Johns Hopkins University. Johnson looked up when Church appeared and said, with an icy
glare, "How's the dam program coming out in Idaho?" Church replied,
"Mr. President, the next dam we finish, we're going to call the Walter
Lippmann Dam." And Johnson roared with laughter.[28]

A colloquy and debate in the Senate had begun, but time was running
out. Strongly expressed opposition at the time of the Gulf of Tonkin
Resolution might have been effective, but by February plans were already underway not only for the massive bombing but for the introduction of U.S. ground forces.

Senator McGovern relates a sidelight which frightened him. Before he
and Senator Church delivered their February speeches, they showed copies to their old friend, Hubert Humphrey, now the vice-president. Their
intent was to do so as a courtesy to the vice-president. When Humphrey
read them, he was shocked and said, "My God, you can't say that. At
least speak to Bundy first." They agreed, and Bundy was in Humphrey's
office within fifteen minutes. Humphrey obviously intended Bundy to
refute the horrible distortions of the dissenters. But when given the
speech, Bundy began to read, never saying a word while the blood
drained from his face. He finished and left without saying a word. Senator McGovern feels that McNamara and Bundy during those days never
even read the positions of the opponents, and that that is why the substance of the opponents' arguments so shocked him.[29]

Even in his memoirs and confession, McNamara avoids the question
of whether he harbored any doubts at the very outset, during this period.
It seems clear that he did not; nor it appears did Bundy, yet Bundy,
upon reading the speech, must have realized that there was another reasonable side to the Vietnam question, at least.

WAS LBJ CARRYING OUT PRESIDENT KENNEDY'S POLICIES?

Johnson and his advisors consistently maintained that they were following the policy of President Kennedy to stand fast in Vietnam. But

were they? Kennedy showed great ambivalence concerning Vietnam, both in word and in deed. No doubt Johnson's conviction that following John Kennedy's advisors and therefore his policy helped him deal with his inner turmoil and an instinctive feeling that he was being trapped. One way to justify his war policy was to say he was merely following the policy of the Harvards. The belief that Jack Kennedy's policy was still being conducted by his own National Security Advisor and Secretary of Defense probably caused later dissident senators to hold back their public opposition.

What then was President Kennedy's policy in Vietnam? The most accurate analysis is that it was not a single-minded, purposeful policy. It reflected ambiguity and uncertainty on the part of the President. But I believe that by the time of his death, there was a definite policy goal being pursued. The President was well aware of General Douglas MacArthur's admonition that never again should American ground troops be subjected to the endless attrition brought about in Korea. MacArthur himself told this to JFK in a discussion they had in April 1961. The President never forgot that advice.[30]

As a senator, Kennedy delivered a major address in the Senate on April 6, 1954,[31] a month before the fall of Dien Bien Phu. It's unfortunate that not enough attention has been given that speech by historians and prophets of what JFK would have done had he lived. His views were clearly stated and set forth the question of what to do in Vietnam.

Excerpts of those remarks are crucial in determining JFK's original thoughts, when President Eisenhower was about to reject the advice of John Foster Dulles, Arthur Radford, Richard Nixon, and the other interventionists.[32]

[T]he speeches of President Eisenhower, Secretary Dulles and others have left too much unsaid, in my opinion—and what has been left unsaid is the heart of the problem that should concern every citizen. For if the American people are, for the fourth time in this century, to travel the long and tortuous road of war— particularly a war which we now realize would threaten the survival of civilization—then I believe we have a right—a right which we should have hitherto exercised—to inquire in detail into the nature of the struggle in which we may become engaged, and the alternative to such struggle. Without such clarification the general support and success of our policy is endangered.

Inasmuch as Secretary Dulles has rejected, with finality, any suggestion of bargaining on Indochina in exchange for recognition of Red China, those discussions in Geneva which concern that war may center around two basic alternatives.

The first is a negotiated peace, based either upon partition of the area between the forces of the Viet Minh and the French Union, possibly along the 16th parallel; or based upon a coalition government in which Ho Chi Minh is represented. Despite any wishful thinking to the contrary, it should be apparent that the popularity and prevalence of Ho Chi Minh and his following throughout Indochina would cause either partition or a coalition government to result in eventual domination by the Communists.

The second alternative is for the United States to persuade the French to continue their valiant and costly struggle; an alternative which, considering the current state of opinion in France, will be adopted only if the United States pledges increasing support. Secretary Dulles' statement that the "imposition in Southeast Asia of the political system of Communist Russia and its Chinese Communist ally" . . . should be met by united action indicates that it is our policy to give such support; that we will, as observed by the New York Times last Wednesday "fight if necessary to keep Southeast Asia out of their hands." . . .

I think it is important that the Senate and the American people demonstrate their endorsement of Mr. Dulles' objectives, despite our difficulty in ascertaining the full significance of its key phrases.

Certainly, I, for one, favor a policy of a "united action" by many nations whenever necessary to achieve a military and political victory for the free world in that area, realizing full well that it may eventually require some commitment of our manpower.

But to pour money, material, and men into the jungles of Indochina without at least a remote prospect of victory would be dangerously futile and self-destructive. Of course, all discussion of "united action" assumes the inevitability of such victory; but such assumptions are not unlike similar predictions of confidence which have lulled the American people for many years and which, if continued, would present an improper basis for determining the extent of American participation.

Permit me to review briefly some of the statements concerning the progress of the war in that area, and it will be understood why I say that either we have not frankly and fully faced the seriousness of the military situation, or our intelligence estimates and those of the French have been woefully defective.

In February of 1951, for example, the late Brig. Gen. Francis G. Brink, then head of the United States Military Advisory Group, in Indochina, told us of the favorable turn of events in that area as a result of new tactics designed by Gen. Jean de Lattre de Tassigny. In the fall of that same year, General De Lattre himself voiced optimism in his speech before the National Press Club here in Washington; and predicted victory, under certain conditions, in 18 months to 2 years, during his visit to France.

In June of 1952, American and French officials issued a joint communique in Washington expressing the two countries' joint determination to bring the battle to a successful end; and Secretary of State Acheson stated at his press conference that . . .

The military situation appears to be developing favorably. . . . Aggression has been checked and recent indications warrant the view that the tide is now moving in our favor. . . . We can anticipate continued favorable developments.

In March 1953, the French officials again came to Washington, again issued statements predicting victory in Indochina, and again joined with the United States in a communique planning military action and United States support which would achieve their new goal of decisive military victory in 2 years.

Senator Kennedy had described the future Vietnam war with precise detail. Should the United States act unilaterally? He said no. Wasn't there repeated light at the end of the tunnel, as Secretary McNamara argued for the entire early 1960s? Well, so did the French generals ten years earlier and they were all wrong. Kennedy recognized that a negotiated settlement would result in a Viet Minh takeover of the entire people because the people, other than the minority of French supporters, wanted it. But nevertheless Kennedy would not "pour money, material and men into the jungles of Indochina without at least a remote prospect of victory." Senator Kennedy, in his speech, clearly desired that the independence of Vietnam be maintained. But at what price? It is clear that Senator Kennedy, in 1954, understood the reality and futility of winning a land war in Vietnam's jungles. Yet many of his actions upon assuming office appeared to contradict that previous position.

When the Kennedy administration took office in 1961, there were 685 U.S. military advisors in South Vietnam. In the fall of 1961, pursuant to recommendations of Maxwell Taylor and McNamara, 8,000 were added and in the weeks preceding his murder, the President raised the level of military advisors to 16,000.[33]

What was the reason for this seeming change of heart? Did President Kennedy retreat from his policy recommendations of nine years before?

Despite the changes that had taken place in the world between 1954 and 1961, I believe that a strong argument can be made that Kennedy's view of the question of Vietnam did not change. His actions were not a contradiction to his previous statements. The influx of advisors to Vietnam was in part a response to events in other parts of the world that were far more important and grave than Vietnam per se.

According to David Halberstam, even after commitment of the advisors, two important men in Washington had strong misgivings about sending in combat troops. One was John Kennedy, the other was George Ball, Under Secretary of State.[34] When Taylor recommended a commitment of only 8,000 combat troops, Ball told President Kennedy that the commitment would not remain small, that it would rise to 300,000 men in a few years. The President laughed and said, "George, you're crazier than hell." But the President had been shaken.[35]

Senator Richard Russell cautioned the new President in early 1961, "I hope you will take a long, hard look before you commit anybody over there. . . . It would be a festering sore. We'd be still sitting there three or four years from now."[36]

Yet, despite the seemingly hostile acts and Cold War rhetoric, one observes many seemingly contradictory positions and private statements made by the President. At the time the request for more advisors came in, Kennedy told White House aide Arthur Schlesinger, "They want a force of American troops.[37] They say it is necessary in order to restore confidence and morale. But it will be just like Berlin. The troops will march in and in four days everyone will have forgotten. Then we will be told we have to send more troops. It's like taking a drink. The effect wears off and you have to have another."[38]

And so the President's actions and remarks were frequently contradictory. For example, in his last public comments on Vietnam, in an interview with Walter Cronkite on September 2, 1963, he said that our role is only to help, and if their corruption causes defeat, so be it. Yet, large numbers of advisors were being sent, and he must have known they were militarily engaged.

> *The President. I don't think that unless a greater effort is made by the Government to win popular support that the war can be won out there. In the final analysis, it is their war. They are the ones who have to win it or lose it. We can help them, we can give them equipment, we can send our men out there as advisors, but they have to win it, the people of Viet-Nam, against the Communists.*
>
> We are prepared to continue to assist them, but I don't think that the war can be won unless the people support the effort and, in my opinion, in the last two months, the government has gotten out of touch with the people.
>
> The repressions against the Buddhists, we felt, were very unwise. Now all we can do is to make it very clear that we don't think this is the way to win. It is my hope that this will become

increasingly obvious to the government, that they will take steps to try to bring back popular support for this very essential struggle.

Mr. Cronkite. Do you think this government still has time to regain the support of the people?

The President. I do. With changes in policy and perhaps with personnel I think it can. If it doesn't make those changes, I would think that the chances of winning it would not be very good.

Mr. Cronkite. Hasn't every indication from Saigon been that President Diem has no intention of changing his pattern?

The President. If he does not change it, of course, that is his decision. He has been there 10 years and, as I say, he has carried this burden when he has been counted out on a number of occasions.

Our best judgment is that he can't be successful on this basis. We hope that he comes to see that, but in the final analysis it is the people and the government itself who have to win or lose this struggle.[39] [Emphasis added.]

A suggested hypothesis is that President Kennedy's moves in Southeast Asia were in response to the primary threats of the time. It was in early 1961 that Nikita Khrushchev badly misjudged Kennedy at Vienna. The Chairman's threat to conclude a separate German peace treaty with East Germany was a frightening thought, because it would have meant war. We were committed to free access to West Berlin. Being in East Germany, a peace treaty giving the East German regime autonomy was a greater threat than the 1948 blockade when the USSR had no nuclear capability.

In August 1961, the Berlin Wall went up, and Kennedy called up the reserves. Between these events was the debacle of the Bay of Pigs in April. Kennedy's refusal to commit U.S. air power to a lost cause was courageous. There had never been a greater failure in the history of U.S. intelligence than the bungled plans for the Cuban invasion. But to the world, Kennedy's refusal to compound Allen Dulles' incompetence was seen as an act of weakness.

Khrushchev's incredible risk of installing nuclear warheads in Cuba in 1962 was based on his erroneous assessment of President Kennedy's character.

So perhaps the President felt a need to demonstrate his toughness and chose Southeast Asia as the vehicle, for reasons having nothing to do with Vietnam per se. Support for this theory may be drawn from the memoir *Deadline*, by James Reston. Reston spoke with a shaken President Kennedy after one of the Vienna sessions with Khrushchev. Reston wrote, "He had tried to convince Khrushchev of U.S. determination but had failed. It was now essential to demonstrate our firmness and the place to do it, he remarked to my astonishment, was Vietnam. I don't think I swallowed his bait but I was speechless. . . . Khrushchev had treated Kennedy with contempt, and . . . he felt he had to act."[40]

As we have seen from the McNamara seminar, the President, seeing the pressure for American involvement to intensify, would likely have cut his losses after the 1964 election and gotten out, using as a valid pretext the 1954 letter from Eisenhower to President Diem conditioning U.S. aid on internal South Vietnam reforms, which never were fulfilled.

In a discussion with Senate Majority Leader Mansfield, whose opposition to involvement was known, JFK admitted that Mansfield was probably right, and the only solution was a complete military withdrawal. Afterward he told a nearby aide, "If I tried to pull out completely now from Vietnam we would have another Joe McCarthy red scare on our hands, but I can do it after I'm reelected. So we had better make damn sure that I *am* reelected."[41]

I heard former Speaker of the House Tip O'Neil remark that the President had told him he'd be out after the 1964 election. Nevertheless, LBJ, I believe, truly thought he was carrying out Kennedy policy and that President Kennedy would have followed every step that he took. Kennedy's staff was with him. At the beginning, the Attorney General—Robert Kennedy, his brother's alter ego—was supportive.

In late 1997, newly declassified documents revealed support of an anecdotal nature of President Kennedy's intention to be out of South Vietnam by the end of 1965. An October 4, 1963, memorandum drafted by the chairman of the Joint Chiefs of Staff, General Taylor, said, "All planning will be directed toward preparing Republic of Vietnam forces for the withdrawal of all United States special assistance units and personnel by the end of calendar year 1965."[42]

NOTES

1. Lloyd Gardner, *Pay Any Price* (Chicago: Ivan R. Dee Publishers, 1995), p. 180.

2. Cong. Rec. S14793 (Daily ed., June 23, 1964).

3. Ibid., S14793–96.

4. Ibid., S18415 (Daily ed., Aug. 6, 1964).

5. Ibid.

6. Ibid.

7. Interview with Senator George McGovern, February 29, 1996.

8. Cong. Rec. S18416 (Daily ed., Aug. 6, 1964).

9. Ibid.

10. Ibid., S18417.

11. Interview with Senator George McGovern, February 29, 1996.

12. Ibid.

13. David Halberstam, *The Best and the Brightest* (New York: Random House, 1969), p. 537; Herbert V. Schandler, *Unmaking of a President: Lyndon Johnson and Vietnam* (Princeton, N.J.: Princeton University Press, 1977), p. 15.

14. Cong. Rec. S2870 (Daily ed., Feb. 17, 1964).

15. Ibid., S2871.

16. Speech is discussed in Chapter 3.

17. *Supra*, 74–75.

18. Cong. Rec. S2870 (Daily ed., Feb. 17, 1964).

19. Ibid., S2880.

20. Ibid.

21. Ibid., S2885.

22. Tom Wells, *The War Within: America's Battle over Vietnam* (Berkeley: University of California Press, 1994), p. 68.

23. Interview with Senator Gaylord Nelson, May 2, 1996.

24. Cong. Rec. S2886 (Daily ed., Feb. 17, 1965).

25. Cong. Rec. S3188 (Daily ed., Feb. 18, 1965).

26. To my knowledge, this episode has never appeared in print. When told of what Dirksen said, Senator Nelson exploded, saying, "Now you've got the most powerful member of the Senate calling me a communist." But as always, the senator never remained angry against staff for more than a minute or two. He thought we were pushing him to an even more extreme position on the war, when actually it was his own courage that carried him. I believe his outburst was merely a reflexive reaction to strike out at the messenger. If I recall correctly, Dirksen had the remark expunged from the *Congressional Record* before it was published. But the episode is a confirmation of the well-earned reputation of Dirksen as a smear artist.

27. LeRoy Ashby and Rodd Cramer, *Fighting the Odds* (Pullman: Washington State University Press, 1994), p. 199.

28. Ibid., pp. 199–201.

29. Interview with Senator George McGovern, February 29, 1996.

30. Theodore C. Sorsenson, *Kennedy* (New York: Bantam, 1966), p. 723.

31. Cong. Rec. S4672 (Daily ed., April 6, 1954). The full text of Senator Kennedy's speech is in Appendix VI.

32. As discussed in Chapter 1.

33. John Prados, *The Hidden History of the Vietnam War* (Chicago: Ivan Dees Publishers, 1993), pp. 3–4.

34. Halberstam, *The Best and the Brightest*, p. 173.

35. Ibid., p. 174.

36. Ibid., pp. 174–75.

37. David M. Barrett, *Uncertain Warriors* (Lawrence: University of Kansas Press, 1993), p. 35.

38. Halberstam, *The Best and the Brightest*, p. 175.

39. John F. Kennedy, *Presidential Papers of the Presidents of the United States*. No. 340, Sept. 2, 1963.

40. Seymour Hersh, *The Dark Side of Camelot* (New York: Little, Brown, 1997), pp. 252–53.

41. Gardner, *Pay Any Price*, pp. 72–73.

42. *Chicago Tribune*, Dec. 23, 1997, p. 12. This news received wide coverage in Europe as well. An English-language press release by Agence France Presse dated December 23, 1997, with the headline, "Kennedy wanted plan to end Vietnam War in 1965," read as follows:

Former U.S. president John Kennedy ordered his advisers to draft a plan to withdraw U.S. forces from Vietnam weeks before he was assassinated, newly declassified documents show.

A memo dated October 4, 1963, from Kennedy's chairman of the joint chiefs of staff Maxwell Taylor said the president has asked for such a plan to be drafted and submitted for review two days earlier.

The document said the plans to end U.S. involvement were to be discussed with South Vietnamese president Ngo Dinh Diem.

But Diem was assassinated just weeks before Kennedy's death November 22, 1963. President Lyndon Johnson stepped up the campaign after assuming the presidency, and U.S. troops remained until 1975.

The memo said U.S. commanders should review plans "to complete the military campaign in the northern and central areas . . . by the end of 1964 and in the (Mekong) Delta . . . by the end of 1965."

It said South Vietnamese forces should be trained to assume "all essential functions . . . by the end of calendar year 1965."

"All planning will be directed towards preparing RVN (South Vietnamese) forces for the withdrawal of all U.S. special assistance units by the end of the calendar year 1965."

5

ROLLING THUNDER

The support in Congress for this measure is clearly overwhelming.
Obviously you need my vote less than I need my conscience.
—Senator Gaylord Nelson[1]

In an analysis by Max Frankel in the *New York Times*, October 2, 1964,
the question of future escalation was discussed. Cited were administration sources who declared that the President had publicly and privately
said that neither U.S. nor South Vietnamese interests would be served
by a big offensive against North Vietnam. Lyndon Johnson feared any
situation that would have American troops face the Chinese army.[2]

The deterioration of the South Vietnamese government, some administration sources argued, must be stopped by some military action of the
United States. Thus far, revealed Frankel, President Johnson had rejected
that advice. William Bundy argued in a speech that limited ground forces
would render the guerrilla threat to manageable proportions "in a matter
of months." At that time of early October, Secretaries Dean Rusk, Robert
McNamara, and General Maxwell Taylor, Ambassador to South Vietnam, were described by Frankel as being "firmly opposed to any expansion of the war for punitive reasons."

The same day, October 2, James Reston wrote a column in the *New
York Times* entitled "What Are Our War Aims in South Vietnam?"

Reston, through his dependable sources, wrote that within the Johnson administration there was currently a debate between some who wished to go North with American ground troops to prevent collapse of the corruption-ridden South Vietnamese government, and the non-interventionists. Reston wrote that some spoke of provoking an incident. In Reston's words, this internal debate "clouds an already complicated and devilish dilemma with suspicion."

Senator Gaylord Nelson responded to these ominous rumors with a letter to the *Times*, which was published October 6. He stressed Fulbright's assurances that the Gulf of Tonkin Resolution did not contemplate a change in the basic American role of advisor and certainly did not intend an authorization of use of American ground forces.[3]

Nevertheless, despite President Johnson's reluctance and misgivings, plans for escalation were made.

The crucial episode was a raid by Viet Cong guerrillas on the U.S. base at Pleiku that occurred 2:00 A.M., February 7, 1965. Eight U.S. personnel were killed and large quantities of equipment were destroyed. Bundy was then in South Vietnam and recommended to the President that Phase II of the previously planned military measures against North Vietnam should be immediately undertaken. The decision to retaliate was made 75 minutes later.[4]

General Taylor remained strongly opposed to the use of ground troops. Even after Pleiku, Taylor stuck to his statement of a year earlier, February 17, 1964, when he was Chairman of the Joint Chiefs of Staff, that "I would oppose the use of United States troops as the direct means of suppressing the guerrillas in South Vietnam."[5] Nevertheless, Taylor supported the bombing,[6] a puzzling position in light of his former superiors in rank and in military tactics, Generals Matthew Ridgway and Dwight Eisenhower, who remained firm in believing that air attacks without ground troops are useless.[7] Ultimately General Taylor, too, agreed that bombing alone would not win the war.

It had taken McNamara, Bundy, and Rusk four months to get Johnson to commit himself to the long-term bombing of Rolling Thunder. But just a few days after Rolling Thunder began on March 2, Mac Bundy told Johnson that McNamara and other experts had been mistaken. Victory would not be achieved through military engagements, but rather through pacification programs from the village up.[8] Mac Bundy urged bombing as the solution upon a reluctant President, then a few days after he agreed, reversed course and decided pacification was the way to go.

As we know, the United States tried both—the bombing continued, and pacification programs were undertaken—but neither worked. There were no leadership, no intelligent, qualified advisors to counsel a befuddled President. Not until the end of his term did Johnson have the sense to consult with Clark Clifford, who had the courage to tell him his policy was a failure. White House aides Mac Bundy and Walt Rostow, and Secretaries Rusk and McNamara were the architects of the failure.

This all confirms the theory that the United States had no real policy in place for the period after the initial August reprisal raids.[9] The Americans blundered ahead day by day, responding to events, with no idea how to reach a specific goal or even what that specific goal was to be. As Senator Nelson expressed it to me, "Let's say we put in the needed number of troops to secure the territory. Then what? Do they stay there forever? No one really was thinking of this."[10]

Rolling Thunder began on March 2, with the first large predetermined air raids on targets in North Vietnam. Senator George McGovern relates that, on the evening of March 5, at 7:30 P.M., he went to the White House to express to Johnson his concern over what was obviously a change in policy. He was worried where this escalation would lead. McGovern asked the President, "What happens if we hit a target you have declared off limits, such as a Soviet ship?" Johnson replied, "Don't worry about that, my boys don't hit a shit house unless I tell them." Senator McGovern, 31 years later, recalled "those were his exact words."[11]

Despite the obvious escalation of the war, it seemed to maintain public support, and more importantly, J. William Fulbright continued to support administration policy. In February 1964, he stated in a speech that he was agreeable "Whether we seek a general negotiation without first trying to alter the military situation, or whether the war is carried to the territory of North Vietnam with a view to negotiating a reasonable settlement."[12]

This was precisely the policy President Johnson adopted a year later, in February 1965, with his approval of Rolling Thunder. This explains why, as Fulbright later turned on administration policy, Johnson regarded it as a personal betrayal, and why his personal animosity was turned on Fulbright and not on Wayne Morse, who was consistent throughout. Fulbright's continued support, though, in February and March 1965 was a significant additional factor in senatorial silence.

During those early months of his administration, Johnson's Great Society program was introduced in Congress, and it appeared that the overwhelming Democratic majority would enact the whole package. The Voting Rights Bill was about to pass, the most significant Civil Rights Legislation since the Civil War. Yet, while his most precious, long dreamed-of successes were about to become reality, Johnson was sinking into the quicksand of an Asian land war, knowing down deep that his beloved Great Society would be the first casualty.

The success of Rolling Thunder militarily was highly questionable. As an example, Senator Morse, on April 8, cited that the day before 35 jet aircraft dropped 20 tons of rockets and napalm, resulting in the destruction of seven trucks and damage to four others—two tons of bombs per truck.[13]

Strategically, the value of the bombing was also questioned. The following dialogue between Secretary McNamara and Senator Sam Ervin took place in hearings of February 1965.

> *Secretary McNamara.* The industry in the north is so small that it plays a very little role in the economy of the north, and I think any of the analysts who have studied the problem would say it could be completely eliminated and not reduce in any substantial way the contribution from the North to South Vietnam.
>
> *Senator Ervin.* And you are telling us, am I to infer, that you could wipe out the entire industry of North Vietnam, and have no effect whatever upon their capability to prosecute the war?
>
> *Secretary McNamara.* It might affect their will to do so. In my opinion, it would have no measurable effect upon their capability to furnish the supplies they are presently supplying to the Communist forces in South Vietnam.
>
> *Senator Ervin.* What do they do with their oil and gasoline that comes in?
>
> *Secretary McNamara.* Yes—they use it for the operation of their aircraft which, so far, have played practically no role in combat operations in North Vietnam. They use it for fuel for their trucks, some of which are used on the infiltration routes.
>
> The portion of fuel used by their trucks could be obtained even though we were to mine the Haiphong and Gon Gai harbors. And, if they got no fuel for trucks, they have demonstrated many, many times before that, in the Orient, they can move the quantities of supplies now being moved into the South by animal and manpower.
>
> *Senator Ervin.* Well, it would seem that North Vietnam is entirely unessential to this war, according to your testimony.
>
> *Secretary McNamara.* No. It is not unessential. They are supplying the leadership, they are supplying the cadres, they are moving the equipment obtained from other Communist countries.
>
> *Senator Ervin.* Don't you think a massive air attack on North Vietnam would have a vast effect on the will of the people to continue to fight?
>
> *Secretary McNamara.* No one can be sure how they would react. I do not believe that it did in Japan, and I do not believe that it did in World War II, and I do not believe it did in Korea.
>
> I think a study of the record will show that massive air power

by itself did not break the will of the people nor did it break the
will of their political leaders.

It was airpower, massive airpower complemented by ground
and sea action, that broke the will of the people and their leaders.[14]

And so, in closed Senate testimony, McNamara as early as February
1965 admitted the inadequacy of the bombing alone and stressed the
need for accompanying ground troops—all this before Rolling Thunder
had even begun.

Senator Nelson relates a revealing side note to the purpose and success
of the bombing campaign. The Air Force was under strict orders not to
hit Hanoi or Haiphong, but it was taking out bridges and railroads.
Repairs were undertaken by Chinese workers.

CIA Director Richard Helms, in briefing Nelson, Senator George Mc-
Govern, and Senator Edward Kennedy, said that they were bombing
bridges and railroad tracks and some brick factories, but all essential
material was being brought down from the North on people's backs.
Nelson then asked if there were therefore nothing really worth bombing,
and mentioned this to Senator Stuart Symington (D.-Mo.), a strong advocate of the bombing. Symington told Nelson that it was not so, and
that he would speak with Helms. Nelson concluded by saying, "However, when he, like a number of others, finally saw that the cause was
lost, the excuse they all gave was that if we are not going to win the war
there, we might as well get out, and we aren't doing enough to win, we
have dropped more bombs on North Vietnam than we did on all of
Europe, but at any rate McNamara was there and they had the maps
up, they had bombed those bridges but they weren't down, we couldn't
see [on the airial photos] where there was a hole there. [Now] they
weren't using them but . . . Johnson said can't those pilots do any better
than that, fly over there with no challenge and they can't knock down a
bridge, what's wrong with them?"[15]

THE JOHNS HOPKINS UNIVERSITY SPEECH

On April 7, 1965, Senators Frank Church, George McGovern, and Gale
McGee were summoned at 5:00 P.M. to the White House. Senator
McGee's presence was a bit mysterious, since he was an all-out hawk.
McGeorge Bundy gave them copies of the speech the President would
deliver that evening at the Johns Hopkins University in Baltimore. A
quick glance at the text showed that the President was going to make
reference to negotiations.

Bundy then took them upstairs to meet with the President, who said
"Now, I'm doing exactly what you fellers wanted me to do. I'm going

to offer to negotiate."[16] Yet as Senator McGovern later said with disappointment, the offer of "unconditional negotiations" had so many conditions attached as to render negotiations impossible.[17]

On April 7, 1965, Johnson delivered his Johns Hopkins speech in Baltimore. Circumstances surrounding the speech were bizarre and inexplicable. The address was intended to be a statement of U.S. policy in Vietnam. Close examination of the speech reveals the hand of Johnson, but how could his "brilliant advisors" allow such a contradictory document to be issued as a statement of American policy?

> Tonight Americans and Asians are dying for a world where each people may choose its own path to change.
> This is the principle for which our ancestors fought in the valleys of Pennsylvania. It is the principle for which our sons fight tonight in the jungles of Viet-Nam . . .
> . . . THE NATURE OF THE CONFLICT
> The world as it is in Asia is not a serene or peaceful place.
> The first reality is that North Viet-Nam has attacked the independent nation of South Viet-Nam. Its object is total conquest.
> Of course, some of the people of South Viet-Nam are participating in the attack on their own government. But trained men and supplies, orders and arms, flow in a constant stream from north to south.
> This support is the heartbeat of the war.
> And it is a war of unparalleled brutality.[18]

Thus, it was a total rejection of any thought that really the Vietnam war was an indigenous rebellion by the Viet Cong in the South to reunite with the former Viet Minh in the North, against a minority of those who had opposed Ho Chi Minh and supported the French since 1945.

> Over this war—and all Asia—is another reality: the deepening shadow of Communist China. The rulers in Hanoi are urged on by Peking. This is a regime which has destroyed freedom in Tibet, which has attacked India, and has been condemned by the United Nations for aggression in Korea. It is a nation which is helping the forces of violence in almost every continent. The contest in Viet-Nam is part of a wider pattern of aggressive purposes.[19]

Vietnam is as Tibet? China casts a shadow? In reality it was the Soviet Union that supplied the Vietnamese communists, and the analogy to Tibet is foolish, since in Tibet there was no support for the Chinese presence and indeed it was an act of pure aggression. Did Mac Bundy, former Dean of Harvard College, see and approve of this text? According to the notes printed in Presidential Paper number 172 for 1965 he did.

WHY ARE WE IN VIET-NAM?

Why are these realities our concern?

Why are we in South Viet-Nam?

We are there because we have a promise to keep. Since 1954 every American President has offered support to the people of South Viet-Nam. We have helped to build, and we have helped to defend. Thus, over many years, we have made a national pledge to help South Viet-Nam defend its independence.

And I intend to keep that promise.[20]

The pledge to aid the South Vietnamese by President Eisenhower did not include military participation by the United States. It was based upon the promise that South Vietnam would enact democratic reforms and eliminate corruption. None of this had happened.

We are also there because there are great stakes in the balance. Let no one think for a moment that retreat from Viet-Nam would bring an end to conflict. The battle would be renewed in one country and then another. The central lesson of our time is that the appetite of aggression is never satisfied. To withdraw from one battlefield means only to prepare for the next. We must say in southeast Asia—as we did in Europe—in the words of the Bible: "Hitherto shalt thou come, but no further."

There are those who say that all our effort there will be futile— that China's power is such that it is bound to dominate all southeast Asia. But there is no end to that argument until all of the nations of Asia are swallowed up.

There are those who wonder why we have a responsibility there. Well, we have it there for the same reason that we have a responsibility for the defense of Europe. World War II was fought in both Europe and Asia, and when it ended we found ourselves with continued responsibility for the defense of freedom.[21]

This was more of Secretary McNamara's dominoes from his March 1964 speech. Vietnam was equated with Europe.

The first part of the speech was the stick, which was then followed by a very large carrot, reflecting total ignorance of the history of the Vietnamese civil war. After the belligerent tone of the beginning of the speech, Johnson shifted gears and made his offer to negotiate and to rebuild Vietnam, just as he had promised Senators Frank Church and McGovern. He neglected to tell them, though, of the threat that accompanied the generosity of his offer.

In exchange for North Vietnam to close its assistance to the Viet Cong, the President promised massive economic help.

> For our part I will ask the Congress to join in a billion dollar American investment in this effort as soon as it is underway.
>
> And I would hope that all other industrialized countries, including the Soviet Union, will join in this effort to replace despair with hope, and terror with progress.
>
> The task is nothing less than to enrich the hopes and the existence of more than a hundred million people. And there is much to be done.
>
> The vast Mekong River can provide food and water and power on a scale to dwarf even our own TVA.[22]

This seems to be vintage LBJ from back in the Senate days. You give me what I want and I'll give you a TVA. Was this merely breathtaking naivete or a calculated offer he knew would be rejected, but which would silence the Senate opponents?

> A dam built across a great river is impressive.
>
> In the countryside where I was born, and where I live, I have seen the night illuminated, and the kitchens warmed, and the homes heated, where once the cheerless night and the ceaseless cold held sway. And all this happened because electricity came to our area along the humming wires of the REA. Electrification of the countryside—yes, that, too, is impressive.
>
> A rich harvest in a hungry land is impressive.
>
> The sight of healthy children in a classroom is impressive.
>
> These—not mighty arms—are the achievements which the American Nation believes to be impressive.
>
> And, if we are steadfast, the time may come when all other nations will also find it so.

There can be no doubt who the author of those lines was. And he probably meant it.

Predictably Senate reaction to the speech varied. Mike Mansfield's guarded response reveals a restrained skepticism. "We are at crossroads in Vietnam . . . the entire world trembles at it."[23] The Majority Leader asked for a new Geneva conference, which is, of course, precisely what the administration did not want.

Senator Church, the articulate opponent of U.S. policy, announced that he "was not much encouraged by the speech."[24] However, he thought the offer to develop the Mekong River project a fine idea.

Johnson supporters at least showed more intellectual honesty in their responses. Senator Smathers (D.-Fla.) made it clear that "the iron hand in the velvet glove is an old principle of statesmanship."[25] As we have seen, the number of senators critical of administration policy was slowly growing. Why did not anyone have the fortitude to stand and say that the whole Hopkins proposal of stick and carrot, bombing and killing, and in exchange for a TVA, was a sham? Johnson may well have thought he was acting reasonably and in good faith. He was being sucked into the war he did not want. Use of ground troops was already decided upon within the administration. As Under Secretary George Ball said, Johnson had no knowledge of foreign countries or their people, so perhaps he believed that after fighting Western occupation for twenty years, Ho Chi Minh would cash it all in for the bill of economic aid. The offer was again vintage LBJ the Senate majority leader, you vote for my state textile industry to have open shops and I'll give you your TVA. He just did not understand that Ho Chi Minh and Vo Nguyen Giap were not Everett Dirksen and Bob Kerr. And so it fell again to Wayne Morse to describe the speech and its true meaning with accuracy.

Mr. President, the President's speech of last night is being described as the carrot that goes with the stick, the offer and the promise to go with the use of force. Presumably, the air raids on the North were designed to force North Vietnam to a conference table more or less on our terms.

Now, so the argument goes, we can say that we have offered to negotiate a peace and if the offer is not accepted it is the fault of someone else, not the United States.

Yet 2 months ago, when the air raids on the North began, American voices were saying that we had to step up our military activity so that we could bargain at the conference table from a position of strength. How often that phrase has been thrown out in Washington in the last few months. But I have never heard any explanation of why it is a policy that only our side could or should adopt.

Is anyone going to say now that North Vietnam should not undertake any negotiations from a position of weakness, but should increase her own military activity so that when any negotiations do begin, she can bargain from a position of strength?

I heard nothing in the President's speech that suggests to me he has any negotiations in mind at all. There was a lot of lip-service paid to the theory of peace, grandiose utopian verbiage was plentiful, and the dollar sign was liberally displayed, apparently in hopes of quieting criticism from abroad. But there was no language that suggested that the United States is going to return to the rule of law in southeast Asia or that we are actively seeking a peaceful solution to its problems. There was no word that the United States plans henceforth to observe either the United Nation Charter or the Geneva Agreement of 1954.

All I heard in the President's speech was the United States is going to continue shooting fish in the barrel until they are all dead. *And yesterday 35 jet aircraft dropped 20 tons of rockets and napalm on a mission that resulted in the destruction of 7 trucks and the damaging of 4 others. That is roughly 2 tons of bombs per truck and it makes me wonder if we are not already running out of targets.*

One cannot read that address of last night without being struck by the peculiar shifting description of who we are fighting in Vietnam. In one place we read that: "The first reality is that North Vietnam has attacked the independent nation of South Vietnam."

Several paragraph later we read that it is the deepening shadow of Communist China that is urging on the rulers in Hanoi.

Yet the enemy that the United States must deal with if there are to be any peace negotiations for South Vietnam are the rebels within South Vietnam. They control much of the territory and much of the population of the south. In many districts they operate all the functions of government.

We will not have any real negotiations until we talk to the people we are fighting, and we will not have a genuine offer to negotiate from the White House until the offer is directed to the people we are fighting and not the shadows behind them.

In short, what the President did not say was far more meaningful and significant than what he did say. He did not mention the peacekeeping functions and duties of the United Nations, nor the obligations of the United States under the United Nations Charter. He did not mention that South Vietnam refused to hold the elections in 1956 which were supposed to reunite Vietnam under one government. The most meaningful negotiations that could be held with the north are those that were supposed to have taken place in 1956 to decide the details of a countrywide election.[26] [Emphasis added]

Senator Ernest Gruening said, "If—as the President contends—Hanoi is running the war in South Vietnam, it is difficult to see how the offer of economic aid can constitute anything less than a bribe."[27]

The extreme hawks were ecstatic. Columnist Joe Alsop, gushing over with enthusiasm, wrote:

> The President's great speech of the Vietnamese war was vintage Lyndon B. Johnson [as I have already noted, but my observation was not intended to be complimentary].
>
> The man is so mysterious, so outside the common run of experience, precisely because qualities are mingled in him that in other men are flat opposite. Noble aims do not often go together with extreme craftiness, yet the speech exhibited the President pursuing the noblest aims in the craftiest imaginable manner.[28]

Mike Mansfield continued to be an enigma. His views were against the war in private, yet he attacked Senator Morse's criticism of the speech without naming Morse. He said, "Mr. President, it is most disturbing to find inferences appearing in the wake of the President's recent speech on Vietnam, to the effect that he is trying to buy peace in Vietnam. Any such interpretation of the remarks which he made at Johns Hopkins the other night is entirely unjustified and completely misleading."[29]

Mansfield's closest friend in the Senate was Senator George Aiken (R.-Vt.). Aiken stated the issue facing the President after the speech with wisdom and precision.

> It is plainly evident now that unless reason returns to the world, we will be headed into the most devastating conflict the world has ever known, and we will not come out of it covered with glory, no matter who wins, because no one can win that kind of war.
>
> It is difficult for me to understand what our Armed Forces, our Defense Department, and our executive branch are thinking of when they send 200 planes to blow up a bridge. It is simply braggadocio, our way of saying that this is what we are doing as an example, and it is nothing at all to what we will do if those people of North Vietnam do not yield.
>
> Those people over there, I suppose, are not in a mood to negotiate when they see everything they have worked for being blown to pieces by a huge air fleet. Instead of capitulating they seem to be consumed by greater hatred for the United States.[30]

So despite the increasing number of senators who were developing doubts about the Johnson war policy, few were speaking out. It must be remembered that Johnson was then at the height of his domestic popularity. The programs of the Great Society were being brought before Congress with excellent chances of passage, unscathed by crippling Republican amendments. The war was to the public, it seemed, a mere distraction. American troops were not fighting on the ground. Air Force casualties were very low.

In the weeks following the Johns Hopkins speech, plans intensified for the introduction of ground troops. McNamara gave a briefing to *New York Times* columnist Arthur Krock at the Pentagon. Under the rules, Krock could not say from whom his information came, only that it was from "high government sources." McNamara spoke of U.S. options in Vietnam. What McNamara did not reveal to Krock was that he viewed the war not as an indigenous rebellion, but as a war controlled by forces of North Vietnam that would justify American intervention on the ground. The military was advising use of 100,000 troops, but LBJ was concerned about Ambassador Maxwell Taylor's continued strong opposition to use of ground troops.[31] A week before the Hopkins speech LBJ told his advisors, "If we can just get our feet on their neck."[32] However, no one knew how to do it.

On June 7, LBJ received a cable from General William Westmoreland requesting 125,000 more ground troops. The President could no longer stall. His greatest fear had come to pass. Was this to be another Korea? Would there be Chinese intervention? Finally, at a July 28 press conference, Johnson announced the commitment of ground troops, despite fears of a Korea by Mansfield, Fulbright, and Richard Russell. Russell stated to the President that the real issue was "how to get out and save face."

At the end of 1964, Jack Raymond had written an article about the Church speeches, in the *New York Times*.[33] He listed Democratic senators he thought to be critical of Vietnam policy. This was before Rolling Thunder and long before the Johns Hopkins speech. Besides Senator Church, he listed Senators Mike Mansfield, of Montana, who was majority leader; Ernest Gruening, Alaska; J. William Fulbright, of Arkansas; Wayne Morse, of Oregon; E. L. Bartlett, of Alaska; Claiborne Pell, of Rhode Island, and Gaylord Nelson, of Wisconsin. The listing of Fulbright was an error, since in late 1964 Fulbright was still an administration supporter. Raymond was also obviously unaware of Senator Richard Russell's opposition, because Russell refused to oppose the President publicly.

Of these legislators, Senators Gruening and Morse would have liked to have seen U.S. forces withdrawn from Vietnam immediately. Senator Mansfield argued for considering neutralization, similar to the proposal of Senator Church, as favored by President de Gaulle of France. Senator McGovern proposed a fourteen-nation conference to seek a political settlement in South Vietnam.

Many observers believed that a major foreign policy debate was building up for the next session of Congress and that it would be unusual in that most of the heavy opposition to the administration policies might come from Democrats. The doubts among the senators appear to have developed on the basis of personal studies and judgments. Senator Church's office, for example, said in answer to an inquiry that he had received very little mail on the subject from his constituents.

THE $700 MILLION SUPPLEMENTAL APPROPRIATION BILL

Senator Nelson relates how he first heard of the President's message to Congress for a $700 million supplemental military bill for the Vietnam War exclusively. "I got a call from [Bob] Kastenmeir, [a liberal Democratic Congressman from Milwaukee] and it was, oh, two or three in the afternoon and he said we have a resolution." This was on May 4, 1965. Nelson continued that Kastenmeir thought "it is going to go right through this house to appropriate $700 million for Vietnam," and he said it's recommended out of committee; he said there is not even a committee report or explanation of it. What are you going to do? he said to me. "Well," I said, "this is the first I have heard about it, but if indeed that is what they are proposing I will write a statement. If I can write a statement that will stand up politically."[34]

The introduction of H.J. Res. 447, as the bill was called, and the manner in which it passed was, again, vintage Johnson; practically no hearings, out of committee before most members even knew about it, no real full debate, and a done thing.

This time, however, there was an additional element in the President's accompanying message. A tone of bitterness and challenge to the increasing number of senators who began to oppose the Vietnam War policies. The Presidential message began:

I ask the Congress to appropriate at the earliest possible moment an additional $700 million to meet mounting military requirements in Vietnam.

This is not a routine appropriation. For each Member of Congress who supports this request is also voting to persist in our effort to halt Communist aggression in South Vietnam. Each is saying that the Congress and the President stand united before the world in joint determination that the independence of South Vietnam shall be preserved and Communist attack will not succeed.

Nor can I guarantee this will be the last request. If our need expands I will turn again to the Congress. For we will do whatever must be done to insure the safety of South Vietnam from aggression. This is the firm and irrevocable commitment of our people and nation.

> I have reviewed the situation in Vietnam many times with the Congress, the American people and the world. South Vietnam has been attacked by North Vietnam. It has asked our help. We are giving that help because our commitments, pure principles, and our national interest demand it.

Herein lay true deception and lies. Johnson had not reviewed the Vietnam question with Congress "many times." When? There was the message that accompanied the Gulf of Tonkin Resolution. Isolated private conversation with senators and House members aren't a "review" with Congress. In denying the indigenous nature of the war the President was merely following what his advisors mistakenly believed.

> All of this shrouds battle in confusion. But this is the face of war in the 1960s. This is the "war of liberation." Kept from direct attack by American power, unable to win a free election in any country, those who seek to expand communism by force now use subversion and terror. In this effort they often enlist nationals of the countries they wish to conquer. But it is not civil war. It is sustained by power and resources from without. The very object of this tactic is to create the appearance of an internal revolt and to mask aggression. In this way, they hope to avoid confrontation with American resolution.

Johnson's position is a repeat of McNamara's theory described in his March 1964 speech.

> But we will not be fooled or deceived, in Vietnam or any place in the world where we have a commitment. This kind of war is war against the independence of nations. And we will meet it, as we have met other shifting dangers for more than a generation.
>
> Our commitment to South Vietnam is nourished by a quarter century of history. It rests on solemn treaties, the demands of principle, and the necessities of American security.
>
> A quarter century ago it became apparent that the United States stood between those who wished to dominate an entire continent and the peoples they sought to conquer.
>
> It was our determined purpose to help protect the independence of the Asian peoples.

Could any intelligent, rational person with knowledge of history compare Vietnam with the Japanese imperialism of the Greater East Asia Co-Prosperity sphere? Even a dean of Harvard College must have had a tough time going along with that theory.

That principle soon received another test in the fire of war. And we fought in Korea, so that South Korea might remain free.

Now, in Vietnam, we pursue the same principle which has infused American action in the Far East for a quarter of a century.

The President, whose greatest fear was being trapped in another Korea, now was using the Korean war as an analogy and example of his goals in Vietnam. The most significant section of the Presidential message followed. He said, in effect, that there are senators who claim they didn't know what the significance of the Gulf of Tonkin Resolution vote was. Well, said Johnson in the May 4 message, here it is in black and white. We're out to stop communist aggression as in Greece, Turkey, and Korea.

So this time let there be no mistake what you are voting on. You are voting to support administration policy in Vietnam.

Less than a year ago, the Congress, by an almost unanimous vote, said that the United States was ready to take all necessary steps to meet its obligations under that treaty.

That resolution of the Congress expressed support for the policies of the administration to help the people of South Vietnam against attack—a policy established by two previous Presidents.

Thus, we cannot, and will not, withdraw or be defeated. The stakes are too high, the commitment too deep, the lessons of history too plain.

At every turning point in the last 30 years, there have been those who opposed a firm stand against aggression. They have always been wrong. And when we heeded their cries, when we gave in, the consequences has been more bloodshed and wider war.

Further deception was executed by not mentioning a word in the message that plans were well under way for introduction of ground troops within two months.[35]

In opposition to the appropriation the small minority of Senators Morse, Gruening, and Nelson raised a new constitutional issue. Senator Gruening spoke first.

Mr. President, in his message to the Congress on May 4, 1965, requesting this supplemental appropriation of $700 million to conduct the undeclared war in Vietnam, President Johnson frankly stated that this request was being used not because moneys were needed to supply our Armed Forces in Vietnam, but rather as a vehicle to secure congressional approval of his carrying on the declared war to North Vietnam and anywhere else in southeast Asia that he sees fit.

This the President made clear at the outset of his message when he stated: "This is not a routine appropriation. For each Member of Congress who supports this request is also voting to persist in our effort to halt Communist aggression in South Vietnam. Each is saying that the Congress and the President stand united before the world in joint determination that the independence of South Vietnam shall be preserved and Communist attack will not succeed."[36]

Article I, §9, of the Constitution provides that Congress has the power to appropriate funds. Therefore, argued Senator Gruening, substantive policy can be changed by refusal of Congress to appropriate funds for the continuance of that policy. Senator Gruening continued: "This requested appropriation coupled with the President's message, is in fact tantamount to giving the President a second blank check. . . . I feel strongly that this cannot be done under the Constitution."[37]

But the opponents never really had a chance. There was, as before, limited time allowed for discussion and debate. This time it was five hours.

As I. F. Stone expressed it:

> The way the President's $700,000,000 appropriation for Vietnam was put through the Congress bore the earmarks of a master manipulator. The money by his own admission was not needed; what he wanted was a blank check of authority to widen the war as he saw fit. He could have asked such authority directly. But then the resolution would have been a naked request for war powers and it would have had to go through the Senate Foreign Relations Committee. Its chairman, Fulbright, and at least eight others of its members have grown critical of the expanding war. The grant of power was wrapped in a request for military funds so it would pass through the less critical Senate Appropriations Committee and because it is difficult to vote against supplies for troops on the firing line.

Only three Senators, Morse, Gruening, and Gaylord Nelson of Wisconsin voted "no." Many of those who voted "yes" indicated their misgivings. But fear of White House displeasure proved stronger. As we began the descent into what may become one of history's greatest catastrophes, political cowardice won out over conscience. Even Stennis of Mississippi, who was floor manager for the Administration, admitted after Morse's great speech in opposition that Morse was "brilliant" and had raised "some serious points." Not a single Democrat rose to protest when Morse said Johnson was following Goldwater's course. Four Republicans expressed anxiety. Javits objected to "sneaking in" an authorization for combat troops via an appropriation bill; Cooper of Kentucky and Carlson of Kansas urge more effort at negotiations; Aiken of Vermont opposed the bombing in February. Church of Idaho, Pell of Rhode Island and Clark of Pennsylvania indicated that they were voting "yes" with reluctance; Clark urged negotiations with the Viet Cong and a gradual cessation of bombing the North.

The surprise of this lopsided "debate" came in its closing moments when Robert Kennedy of New York for the first time spoke out on foreign policy. He said he was voting for the resolution because Senator Stennis had assured the Senate (but very equivocally) that this was "not a blank check." He said he thought "our efforts for peace should continue with the same intensity as our efforts in the military field" and that we had "erred for some time in regarding Vietnam as purely a military problem."[38]

The old LBJ tactic of ramming legislation through without proper hearings, or floor debate with unanimous consent time restraint was at work again. Senator Joseph Clark (D.-Pa.) expressed his criticism of the process . . .

> The speed with which this request was approved by both Appropriations Committee on Wednesday, May 5, passed by the House and brought to the floor of the Senate under a time limitation which limits debate to 5 hours, makes the determination of this serious judgment much more difficult. We have not been given the time necessary to properly consider the President's request. I regret that the *bipartisan* leadership has undertaken to press us to a decision in such undue and quite unnecessary haste.[39]

With eloquence and courage, Senator Nelson stated his position. His remarks were an objection to the way the major legislation was rammed through, with no deliberation or debate.

> *Mr. Nelson.* Mr. President, in the cloakrooms and on the floor, numerous distinguished Senators from both sides of the aisle have expressed their concern over the precipitate manner in which we are disposing of this matter.
>
> I have no notion what the President said to the majority and minority leadership at the White House. If he requested that this bill be passed this week within a 24-hour period, instead of next week after ample discussion, I have not been so advised. Though

I have a very high regard and respect for the integrity, the patriotism, and the genuine statesmanship of the leadership on both sides of the aisle, I do not intend lightly to delegate my vote to anyone in support of any proposal.

My objection does not run to the merits of this appropriation no matter what the variances of viewpoint, we all know this money will be needed in the future and will be spent. Yet, I think I speak accurately when I say that a very substantial number of this body is gravely troubled by the unseemly haste of our action here today. We all know that our military planning is not so faulty that we need this appropriation right now. If it were required today our very able Secretary of Defense would have urged action quite some time ago.

My dissent is based upon the conviction that when a matter of this import is before us we owe it to ourselves and the nation to discuss it deliberately and fully. That we may all end up agreeing on this particular measure does not detract from the importance of conducting the dialogue. There is a continuing public confusion about where we are going and why. Silence contributes to that confusion. Our branch of the government has its own obligation. We should not default in that obligation, nor should we even give the appearance of doing so. Because of what appears to be a necessity for exceptionally speedy action on a large appropriation, there are many who will conclude that we must be intending to support or endorse a substantial expansion of our role in Vietnam, if not a fundamental change in our mission there. I am sure that neither the Congress nor the President intends consciously that. Nevertheless, you will see that interpretation put on our action from any number of sources within the next few days. I decline to lend my name in any way to that kind of misinterpretation.

The Presiding Officer. The time of the Senator has expired.

Mr. Morse. Mr. President, I yield 1 additional minute to the senator from Wisconsin.

The Presiding Officer. The Senator from Wisconsin is recognized for 1 additional minute.

Mr. Nelson. Mr. President, thus, at a time in history when the Senate should be vindicating its historic reputation as the greatest deliberative body in the world we are stumbling over each other to see who can say "yea" the quickest and the loudest. I regret it, and I think someday we shall all regret it.

Now in the gentlest way I know how I mention to this body that as of this very moment I have yet to receive a call from the leadership or any other source in government advising me of the grave necessity for instant action. I should think if this matter were really so urgent a 15-minute party caucus would have sufficed at least to advise us so.

Thus, reluctantly, I express my opposition to our procedure here by voting "nay." The support in the Congress for this measure is clearly overwhelming. Obviously you need my vote less than I need my conscience.[40] [Emphasis added]

Almost a year later, Senator Nelson expressed similarly simple but eloquent thoughts. It was a time when Senator Fulbright expressed regret for having rejected the Nelson amendment to the Gulf of Tonkin Resolution.

Mr. Fulbright. Mr. President, will the Senator from Wisconsin yield just briefly?

Mr. Nelson. I am glad to yield to the Senator from Arkansas.

Mr. Fulbright. First, I appreciate what the Senator said. I have already said publicly that I believe one of the most serious mistakes I have made as chairman was in not accepting or urging the Senate to accept the amendment offered by the Senator from Wisconsin in August 1964. I do not believe it is proper, and do not wish to take the time to explain the circumstances of that particular moment, but, nevertheless, I believe it was a mistake and I commend the Senator from Wisconsin for having more foresight than I had at that time, and I think many other Senators, as to the possible significance of that resolution.

He did offer a very sensible, limiting amendment to that resolution, and I regret that we did not have the kind of discussion of it in public at that time that we have had recently. But I do commend the Senator from Wisconsin for his foresightedness and regret that I did not have as much.

Mr. Nelson. I believe that the Senator advised me at that time that his interpretation of the resolution was the same as the purpose of my amendment, and that therefore the amendment was unnecessary.

Mr. Fulbright. I thought it was.

Mr. Nelson. I also wish to commend those who have participated in this debate on both sides of the aisle.

Although very frequently I do not agree with the Senator from Oregon, I should like to say that he has made a most valuable contribution to this discussion—and he will continue to do so.

One thing, however, that disturbs me very much is the argument I have heard advanced in the press, by columnists, by distinguished Members of Congress, and people in the executive branch, that we should not be debating this issue because what we say here, in our free country, will be misunderstood by some Communists in some other country, Communists who do not know what free speech is all about and never will.

Mr. President, this is the greatest parliamentary body in the world. It is the oldest parliamentary body in the world. Its function and purpose is constructive debate. The strength of this Nation is measured by its capacity for intelligent debate, not by its ability to goosestep. I hope we do not undermine that source of our power. I have heard it implied here and elsewhere lately that free speech and dissent should stop because it may be misunderstood in Communist countries. This is a dangerous parallel to the theory that was recently used by the Russian court in sentencing two writers to jail, not because of what they said in Russia but in this country which the Russians thought would be misunderstood in America and damage Russia. On that theory the Russian court sentenced the writers to jail.

Over here, we have people saying that we should stop debate because someone else who cannot understand the debate might misunderstand our resolve and damage America.

Mr. President, freedom is what democracy is all about. If some foreign dictator does not understand it, that is too bad. I have no intention of giving up my freedom of speech because some Communist does not understand what free speech is all about—and never will.[41]

Nelson's remarks before passage of H.J. Res. 447 were the statement he'd told Bob Kastenmeir he would write. "I started writing at 3:00 or 3:30 P.M. and wrote until 5:00 and then went home and had supper and then I had a pot of coffee, would you believe it that I sat there puzzling and writing and I didn't go to bed. At 6 o'clock in the morning I went and took a shower and then I headed out at about 7:15, I headed for the office because I had to do a little more touching up. Well it took me 12 hours to put together something [that took 20 minutes to say]."[42]

The ultimate issue came to what the resolution meant. Senator John Stennis, floor manager, stated, "It is not a blank check. I do not believe we are signing a blank check."

The speech delivered by Senator Morse that day is a clear expression of the thesis of this book. He said:

The first point I wish to make is that no matter what semantics Senators use and no matter how much they protest—and they doth [*sic*] protest too much—the fact is that they are abdicating their clear constitutional duties under the Constitution of the United States, for, when they vote for this appropriation, they will again vote to give the President power to make an undeclared war. No Senator and no Representative under the Constitution of the United States has that constitutional authority. Senators can violate their constitutional trust all they desire to. But the senior Senator from Oregon will not be with them. In my judgment, what Senators will do in supporting the request of the President of the United States will be, in effect, action to support the President to continue his own violation of the Constitution of the United States. The President of the United States is acting outside the Constitution in conducting this undeclared war in Asia. Senators seek to give him additional authority, but it is not within their senatorial power, for they cannot delegate the power to make war.

Mr. President, in the interest of saving time, I ask unanimous consent that there be printed at this point in the Record article I, section 8, of the Constitution.

There being no objection, the section was ordered to be printed in the Record, as follows:

Art. I Section 8 The Congress shall have power . . .

　　　　To declare war . . .

Mr. President, that section vests the power to declare war in the Congress; and that is a power that cannot be delegated by a resolution.

PRESIDENT SAYS NEW MONEY NOT NEEDED, ONLY A NEW ENDORSEMENT BY CONGRESS.

The next point I wish to make is that the Senate need not pass this appropriation measure, for the President, from his own lips in the East Room of the White House yesterday, told the members of the committees that he had assembled there that he did not need to ask for an appropriation. From his own lips yesterday the President told Members of Congress assembled that he has the legal authority to transfer the necessary funds. The President then proceeded to tell those assembled why he was doing it in this way.

The President wants to commit Senators again. He told those assembled in the East Room yesterday, in effect, that he wanted them to know that, when they voted for this joint resolution, they would again be committing themselves to support the President's policy in southeast Asia.

In effect the President was, as I've argued before, telling Senators "last year you said you didn't understand what you were voting to do. Now you've had all this time to think about it, so I'll just hold your feet to the fire."[43]

And so, after a winter of increased dissent, awareness, and debate, the Senate caved in completely and H.J. Res. 447 passed 88–3, with only Morse, Gruening, and Nelson voting no.[44]

The May 1965 $700 million supplemental appropriation bill was the point of no return. Deployment of ground troops officially began in July. Escalation took on a life of its own.

Who was to blame for the Senate's collapse at that time? There was Senator Mansfield, an opponent of the war and a person of high integrity and respect, who, as majority leader, allowed the resolution to come over from the House and accepted a five-hour unanimous consent agreement. No real hearings were held. No need for such speed or emergency situation was shown.

Fulbright was beginning to turn, too little, too late.

Lastly, we must come to Senator Russell, prestigious chairman of the Armed Services Committee. His competence in military matters was great, the respect he commanded in the Senate on military questions was unsurpassed. We have seen his dovish views which he held throughout the war. He did not believe in dominos. Had he but told LBJ privately that he would not support the appropriation, it probably wouldn't have been offered. Had he gone public in his opposition, funding for the war would most certainly have been over.

NOTES

1. Cong. Rec. S9754 (Daily ed., May 6, 1965).
2. As discussed in Chapter 1.
3. The full text of Senator Nelson's letter reads:

Letters to the Times
U.S. in Vietnam
Senator Nelson Denies Congress Approved Expansion of War

TO THE EDITOR:

Max Frankel's general story regarding Vietnam and James Reston's specific report [both Oct. 2] that some members of the Administration are urging that our Government "provoke an incident" in the Gulf of Tonkin that would justify an attack on North Vietnam are extremely disturbing.

As the President has said, an expansion of the war would not be in the interests of the United States.

It appears that those within the Administration who urge a change in our policy and a larger involvement in Vietnam have mistaken the intent of Congress in approving a resolution supporting the President's response to provocation in the Gulf of Tonkin in early August. The Congressional resolution endorsed the President's specific action, but, it in no way approved in advance or gave Congressional endorsement to an expansion of the war.

This point has often been misunderstood since some, both in the Congress and in the press, have offered a different interpretation of the resolution.

In colloquy with the Chairman of the Senate Foreign Relations Committee, Senator J. William Fulbright, legislative history was laid down defining this precise point. Although, of course, the Congressional resolution does not limit the President's authority under the Constitution, neither does it offer Congressional endorsement and support for an expanded new course of action.

Amendment Offered

On Aug. 7, on the Senate floor I asked Senator Fulbright whether he could accept the following as an amendment to the resolution.

"The Congress also approves and supports the efforts of the President to bring the problem of peace in Southeast Asia to the Security Council of the United Nations, and the President's declaration that the United States, seeking no extension of the present military conflict, will respond to provocation in a manner that is 'limited and fitting.' Our continuing policy is to limit our role to the provision of aid, training assistance, and military advice, and it is the sense of Congress that, except when provoked to a greater response, we should continue to attempt to avoid a direct military involvement in the Southeast Asian conflict."

Senator Fulbright replied:

"It states fairly accurately what the President has said would be our policy, and what I stated my understanding was as to our policy; also what other Senators have stated."

Because he did not wish to delay approval of the resolution, however, Senator Fulbright could not accept the amendment. Nonetheless, he went on to state:

"I regret that I cannot do it, even though I do not at all disagree with the amendment as a general statement of policy."

Interpretation of Committee

When I suggested to him that others may not have the same understanding of the congressional resolution, Senator Fulbright made it absolutely clear that the Senate Foreign Relations Committee in recommending the resolution viewed it in the same limited sense as the language of my amendment. Senator Fulbright stated:

"Most members of the committee, with one or two exceptions, interpret it the same way."

I would hope that those aides within the Administration who are urging that our Government "provoke an incident" that might expand the war in Vietnam would carefully review the legislative history which defines, limits and interprets the sense of Congress in approving the resolution.

For as I believe most Senators feel, our basic mission in Vietnam is one of providing material support and advice. It is not to substitute our armed forces for those of the South Vietnamese Government, nor to join with them in a land war, nor to fight the war for them.

GAYLORD NELSON,
U.S. Senator from Wisconsin.
Washington, Oct. 2, 1964.

4. Herbert V. Schandler, *The Unmaking of a President* (Princeton, N.J.: Princeton University Press, 1977), p. 12.

5. William G. Effros, *Quotations Vietnam, 1945–1970* (New York: Random House, 1970), p. 21.

6. Lloyd Gardner, *Pay Any Price* (Chicago: Ivan R. Dee Publishers, 1995), p. 181.

7. As discussed in Chapter 1.

8. Gardner, *Pay Any Price*, p. 182.

9. As discussed in Chapter 3.

10. Interview with Senator Gaylord Nelson, May 2, 1996.

11. Interview with Senator George McGovern, February 29, 1996.

12. Isador F. Stone, *In a Time of Torment* (New York: Random House, 1967), p. 340.

13. Cong. Rec. S7498 (Daily ed., April 18, 1965).

14. Inserted into Cong. Rec. S14496 (Daily ed., July 11, 1966) by Senator Wayne Morse.

15. Interview with Senator Gaylord Nelson, May 2, 1996. Direct quote taken from tape of interview.

16. LeRoy Ashby and Rod Cramer, *Fighting the Odds* (Pullman: Washington State University Press, 1994), p. 201.

17. Ibid., p. 202.

18. Lyndon B. Johnson, *Public Papers of the President* (Washington, D.C.: Government Printing Office, 1965), p. 172. The full text of the speech is printed in Appendix VII.

19. Ibid.

20. Ibid.

21. Ibid.

22. Ibid.

23. Cong. Rec. S7493 (Daily ed., April 8, 1965).

24. Ibid., S7494.

25. Ibid., S7496.

26. Ibid., S7497–98.

27. Cong. Rec. S7665 (Daily ed., April 9, 1965).

28. *Washington Post*, editorial pages, April 9, 1965.

29. Cong. Rec. S7805 (Daily ed., April 13, 1965).

30. Cong. Rec. S8125 (Daily ed., April 21, 1965).

31. Gardner, *Pay Any Price*, pp. 201–2.

32. Ibid., p. 202.

33. *New York Times*, December 27, 1964.

34. Interview with Senator Gaylord Nelson, May 2, 1996.

35. The full text of President Johnson's message of May 4, 1965, accompanying H.J. Res. 447, is in Appendix VIII.

36. Cong. Rec. S9729 (May 6, 1965).

37. Ibid., S9731.

38. Stone, *In a Time of Torment*, pp. 232–33.

39. Cong. Rec. S9752 (Daily ed., May 6, 1965) (emphasis added).

40. Ibid., S9759.

41. Cong. Rec. S4378 (Daily ed., March 1, 1966).

42. Interview with Senator Gaylord Nelson, May 2, 1996. A reproduction of part of Nelson's handwritten speech is in the Appendix. The original is in Senator Nelson's archives at the Wisconsin State Historical Society in Madison, Wisconsin.

43. Cong. Rec. S9500 (Daily ed., May 5, 1965). Further remarks of Senator Morse read:

Mr. President, it is a pretty sad thing. In my judgment, we have a President who is worried about being on top of very thin ice so far as American public opinion is concerned. So the

President now wishes Senators to come to his rescue again, as they did last August. He wants Senators again to support him so that he can say, "The Congress by a vote of 500 to 2 endorse my policy." He is using Senators; and that is unfortunate because Senators have some vital questions to which they should have answers from the President of the United States before they fall into this Presidential trap.

I shall answer some of those questions before I finish this part of my speech tonight. But I wish to turn to my third point now.

FOREIGN RELATIONS COMMITTEE OPPOSITION RISING

Last Friday the Foreign Relations Committee met with Secretary Rusk on the situation in Vietnam. It gave the Secretary of State a bad time. The Secretary of State discovered that there was great concern within the Foreign Relations Committee about the overextension of U.S. policies in Vietnam. There were those on that committee protesting the interpretation of the resolution of last August 1964, to the effect that if the interpretation was the interpretation that this administration gave to it, they would not have voted for it.

I say most respectfully that I believe the interpretation of the administration as to what the Congress voted last August is absolutely correct. If Senators wish to extricate themselves from that trap, I say to them, "You ought to insist on certain questions being answered by the President of the United States before you move to support him again with such reservations as you wish semantically to make here on the floor of the Senate."

Listen to what the President in his message has told us:

This is not a routine appropriation. For each Member of Congress who supports this request is also voting to persist in our effort to halt Communist aggression in South Vietnam. Each is saying that the Congress and the President stand united before the world in joint determination that the independence of South Vietnam shall be preserved and Communist attack will not succeed.

If Senators want to know how far the House has gone in making legislative history on the joint resolution, let them read the report that was issued today. The House even goes the President one better in respect to the invitation of the President to have unity on the part of Congress behind him in what I think is a most unfortunate historic mistake my President is making. This what the House report says:

As the President stated in his message of May 4, "This is not a routine appropriation. For each Member of Congress who supports this request is also voting to persist in our effort to halt Communist aggression in South Vietnam."

The House does not intend any verbal reservations to be considered as limiting. I am at a loss to understand the position taken by the administration in seeking to cut domestic expenditures while this trouble is going on. Unfortunately, on both sides of the aisle there are Senators who would like to join in defeating the Great Society domestic program of the President which is in keeping with our obligations under the general welfare clause.

I find myself in the unhappy position of agreeing with the President 99 percent of the time on his domestic program and with much of his foreign policy program. Only on his warmaking program do I disagree. I think the warmaking program is going to be the President's Achilles heel. I believe that in due course of time the American people will repudiate the program and those who support it.

44. Ibid., S9772 (Daily ed., May 6, 1965).

EPILOGUE

"If you send them in they'll get their asses whipped."
  —A reporter to Ambassador to South Vietnam Ellsworth Bunker,
      in reaction to a plan to send South Vietnamese into Laos.[1]

American troop strength peaked at over 500,000 men. The Tet offensive in early 1968, although repelled by the U.S. and South Vietnamese troops, inflicted heavy casualties on our side. General William Westmoreland requested an additional 250,000 troops. Public opinion in middle-class America was turning against the President and the war. Lyndon Johnson ceased appearing among the general public and spoke only at military installations.

President Johnson remarked, after Walter Cronkite turned against the war, that support for the war was finished all through the land. Everyone watched the evening news with Walter Cronkite, on CBS. He formed the opinions of an uncertain middle America.

Following Secretary Robert McNamara's resignation in early 1968, Washington attorney Clark Clifford was appointed Secretary of Defense. Clifford had supported Johnson's policy. When taking office and having the opportunity to study events closely, Clifford later related, "I was convinced that the military course we were pursuing was not only endless, but hopeless. A further substantial increase in American forces

could only increase the devastation and the Americanization of the war.
. . . Henceforth, I was also convinced our primary goal should be to level
off our involvement and to work toward gradual disengagement."[2] Actually, in the summer of 1966, McNamara had recommended to the President that troop levels be cut off at 475,000.

Clifford's conclusions were supported by former Secretary of State
Dean Acheson, heretofore an enthusiastic hawk, George Ball, former Under Secretary of State and opponent of the war, and General Matthew
Ridgway, whose opposition to U.S. participation dated back to 1954.[3]

After receiving Clifford's advice, Johnson, in a nationwide TV address
on March 31, announced only a token troop increase, and de-escalation
of the air war against North Vietnam in order to obtain their entry into
negotiations. At the end of the speech came LBJ's shocking withdrawal
from the 1968 presidential race. Senator Eugene McCarthy (D.-Minn.)
had run a very strong race against Johnson in New Hampshire, and
Senator Robert Kennedy was a declared candidate.[4] Lyndon Johnson had
run out of time.

During the years following the events described in the book, many
attitudes had changed. In an interview, after the war had escalated to
an intense level, Senator J. William Fulbright said:

> Well, if I knew at the time what I know now, I most certainly
> would have made an all-out fight against the adoption of the
> Gulf of Tonkin resolution. . . . I object to it because the basis for
> it was a misrepresentation. In other words, what they alleged as
> the grounds for passing it didn't happen. It was a misrepresentation . . . the President [Johnson] was urging all during that [discussion] that he didn't want a wider war. The resolution was to
> be used to stop the war, not to authorize its expansion. That was
> also a misrepresentation of the President's state of mind, of what
> he was thinking, of what his intentions were. . . .
>
> The President lost touch with reality because he was such an
> efficient manager of the Senate. Having been majority leader and
> having been the protege of Sam Rayburn, he knew how to subvert the Congress and he neutralized and nullified its influence.
> He didn't have the judgment on his own to make the right decisions and he lost contact with the Senate that might have
> helped him if he had allowed it to. But he manipulated it, he
> used his influence to overpower it.[5]

The ultimate negotiated settlement reached by Henry Kissinger in
Paris failed as the North took the entire South by force with a large
measure of assistance from the Southern Viet Cong. This was precisely
the point made by Senator John Kennedy in his April 6, 1954, speech.[6]

Here is a list of Senate votes on Vietnam appropriation bills beginning with the May 6, 1965, $700 million Vietnam Supplemental Appropriation bill. As can be clearly seen, despite the rising opposition to administration policy among the public and in the Senate, when it came to voting, the Senate slept.

May 6, 1965—Vietnam Supplemental Appropriations—Gaylord Nelson, Wayne Morse, and Ernest Gruening voted against (H.J. Res. 440, appropriating $700 million for supplemental emergency funds for S.E. Asia).

March 1, 1967—Vietnam Supplemental Authorization—Nelson and Morse in opposition (S. 665, to authorize $4,467,200,000 in supplemental appropriations).

March 20, 1967—Vietnam Supplemental Appropriations—Nelson, Morse, and Gruening in opposition (H.R. 7123 to provide $12,196,520,000 for the support of military operations in S.E. Asia).

April 19, 1968—Military Procurement Authorization—Nelson, Mike Mansfield, and Gruening in opposition (S. 3292 to authorize appropriations of funds for military procurement and to provide for merging military assistance financing for South Vietnam and other "free world" forces there with the funding for the Department of Defense).

June 25, 1968—Military Construction Authorization—Nelson, Morse, and Stephen Young in opposition (H.R. 16703, authorizing construction at military bases, including $215.1 million for S.E. Asia, and also authorizing the beginning of an ABM system).

June 26, 1968—Proxmire Amendment to H.R. 17734—Nelson and nine others in support (an amendment to eliminate $268 million for B-52 bombing operations in Vietnam for the appropriations).

June 26, 1968—Supplemental Appropriations—Morse and Nelson opposed (H.R. 17734, making supplemental appropriations, including $6.055 million for S.E. Asia Emergency Fund).

July 2, 1968—Supplemental Appropriations—Nelson alone in opposition (H.R. 17734, a conference report on the bill identified above).

August 1, 1968—Military Construction Appropriations—Nelson, Morse, and Young in opposition (H.R. 18785, making appropriations for military construction, including $195,004,00 for South Vietnam and $12.1 million for Thailand).[7]

Senator Nelson, through the years of intensified warfare, continued his critical view of what was occurring. He related to me that after his

first vote against the military appropriations bill, in March 1965, he was
to address an AFL-CIO rally in Milwaukee and was concerned about
what type of reception he'd receive. Labor was for the war, and Nelson
feared he would be badly treated. To his gratification, AFL-CIO leader
Johnny Schmidt, gave him a warm introduction and the crowd ap-
plauded, many coming to him after the speech to express their admira-
tion for his courage in voting his conviction.[8] He was, after all, an old
friend of labor.

Through the years before opposition to the war became widespread,
Nelson continued to speak out. On January 15, 1966 he said:

> The situation is even more dangerous today than it was in May.
> And the pressures to escalate the war are growing in many quar-
> ters. But I believe these cardinal principles should guide our pol-
> icy. Even if a million American soldiers were to force all North
> Vietnamese units from South Viet-Nam and to suppress the Viet
> Cong guerrillas with napalm and bayonets—even if we avoided
> an open clash with Red China—even then, when we withdrew
> as eventually we must, we would leave behind us only a
> charred, desolate country with little hope that it could maintain
> its independence one moment beyond the five we have left out.[9]

That is precisely the point U.S. policy makers missed. Did they think
we could leave soon after "victory"? After 45 years we are still at the
cease-fire line in Korea. Is that what the country had to look forward to?

In a speech on September 1, 1967, more that two years after American
ground forces were engaged—and had—in fact, taken over the primary
combat role—Nelson addressed continued administration reliance on the
Gulf of Tonkin Resolution.

> In recent weeks, there have been renewed and vigorous discus-
> sions about the meaning and intent of the Tonkin Bay Resolu-
> tion. It has lately been repeatedly asserted by Administration
> spokesmen, writers and others that the overwhelming vote for
> the resolution in 1964 expressed Congressional approval of
> whatever future military action the Administration deemed nec-
> essary to thwart aggression in Vietnam including a total change
> in the character of our mission there from one of technical aid
> and assistance to a full scale ground war with our troops.
>
> This, of course, is pure nonsense. If such a proposition had
> been put to the Senate in August 1964, a substantial number of
> Senators, if not a majority, would have opposed the resolution.
> What we are now witnessing is a frantic attempt by the Hawks
> to spread the blame and responsibility for Vietnam on a broader
> base. They should not be allowed to get away with it. It is not

accurate history and it is not healthy for the political system. The future welfare of our country depends upon an understanding of how and why we got involved in a war that does not serve our national self interest. If we don't understand the mistakes that got us into this one, we won't be able to avoid blundering into the next.

For the Administration now to say that the Tonkin Resolution considered during this period had as part of its purpose the intent to secure Congressional approval for fundamentally altering our role in Vietnam to our present ground war commitment is political nonsense if not in fact pure hypocrisy.

If Mr. Fulbright, speaking for the Administration, had in fact asserted that this was one of the objectives of the resolution, the Administration would have repudiated him out of hand. They would have told him and the Congress this resolution had nothing to do with the idea of changing our long established role in Vietnam. They would have told Congress as they were then telling the country that we oppose Goldwater's irresponsible proposals for bombing the North and we oppose getting involved in a land war there with our troops. That was the Administration position when the Tonkin Resolution was before us. They can't change it now. It is rather ironic now to see how many otherwise responsible and thoughtful people have been "taken in" by the line that Congress did in fact by its Tonkin vote authorize this whole vast involvement in Vietnam. The fact is neither Congress nor the Administration thought that was the meaning of Tonkin—and both would have denied it if the issue had been raised.[10]

And on October 21, 1967, Senator Nelson became one of the first doves to directly attack the distortions of the government.

I asked [on August 6, 1964]:

"Am I to understand that it is the sense of Congress that we are saying to the Executive Branch: 'If it becomes necessary to prevent further aggression, we agree now, in advance, that you may land as many divisions as deemed necessary, and engage in a direct military assault on North Vietnam?' "

Of course, I was assured, this was not the purpose of the resolution.

But I wanted to make certain. So we debated this resolution off and on for three days in the Senate. To pinpoint the issue, I offered an amendment making clear that the resolution did not authorize any change in our limited role in Vietnam.

I was assured that the sense of my amendment was embodied in the resolution, that this was the Administration's own interpretation of the resolution. I was urged to withdraw my amendment to avoid the necessity for a conference between the Senate and House on two versions of the resolution.

Now it is true that these assurances came from a man who today is identified as a critic of Administration policies—Senator Fulbright. But in the summer of 1964, he was the Administration's official spokesman on this issue, he managing the Gulf of Tonkin Resolution on the Senate floor. His words were accepted by everyone as faithfully representing the views of the Administration, with which he was in daily contact.

It is even more impressive to speculate on what would have happened if Senator Fulbright had responded differently. What if he had said, in response to my questions:

"This resolution would allow the Administration to decide hereafter whatever steps are necessary in Vietnam. It could be used to justify sending hundreds of thousands of American combat troops to Vietnam, and the launching of massive American air attacks on North Vietnam, right up to the border of China."

Senator Fulbright would have been the most repudiated man in American history. The Administration would have disavowed every word he uttered, for they would have echoed the statements being made by the opposition in the campaign, and they would have shocked the American public.

Secretary [Dean] Rusk says today, "There was no question in anyone's mind as to the meaning of the Gulf of Tonkin Resolution." He is absolutely right. The Senate and the public were assured, and the Administration stood behind those assurances, that the resolution was NOT intended as authorization for escalation of the war.[11]

Nelson's remarks were partially to refute the position taken by then Under Secretary of State Nicholas deB. Katzenbach during testimony before the Senate Foreign Relations Committee in the summer of 1967.

The Under Secretary said that the Administration position was that the Gulf of Tonkin was a major source of its authority to conduct the war. Committee members argued that Johnson had exceeded his authority. Katzenbach replied that in today's world declaration of war was outmoded, especially when fighting for a limited objective, and a Congressional resolution with the 1955 SEATO Treaty was sufficient.[12]

The Vietnam War ended in April 1975. Terms of the negotiated settlement which took from 1968 until 1973 to complete, while the United States sustained tens of thousands of casualties, were repeatedly violated by North Vietnam. Ultimately, they marched in force, captured Saigon, and the South Vietnamese government collapsed. Saigon today is called Ho Chi Minh City.

In his April 1954 speech, Senator John F. Kennedy predicted that this would happen.[13]

It was all for nothing.

NOTES

1. David Halberstam, *The Best and the Brightest* (New York: Random House, 1969), p. 646.

2. Lee R. Powell, *J. William Fulbright and His Time* (Memphis, Tenn.: Guild Bindery Press, 1996), p. 318.

3. Ibid.

4. Ibid., pp. 318–19.

5. Clipping from unknown newspaper, unknown date; surmise it is from late 1960s.

6. The text of Senator Kennedy's 1954 speech is in Appendix VI.

7. Cong. Rec. S21125 (Daily ed., June 24, 1970).

8. Interview with Senator Gaylord Nelson, May 2, 1996.

9. Cong. Rec. S21128 (Daily ed., June 24, 1970).

10. Cong. Rec. S21128–30. These earlier statements were reproduced by Senator Nelson in the Congressional Record of June 24, 1970.

11. Ibid., S21129.

12. E. W. Kenworthy, *New York Times*, August 22, 1967, p. 1. See hearings on U.S. Commitments to Foreign Powers, S. 151, "Is Declaring War Outmoded," testimony by Nicholas deB. Katzenbach, 1967, p. 81, 176.

13. See Appendix VI.

Appendix I

PRESIDENT JOHNSON'S ADDRESS OF AUGUST 4, 1964

My fellow Americans:

As President and Commander in Chief, it is my duty to the American people to report that renewed hostile actions against United States' ships on the high seas in the Gulf of Tonkin have today required me to order the military forces of the United States to take action in reply.

The initial attack on the destroyer *Maddox* on August 2nd was repeated today by a number of hostile vessels attacking two U.S. destroyers with torpedoes. The destroyers and supporting aircraft acted at once on the orders I gave after the initial act of aggression. We believe at least two of the attacking boats were sunk. There were no U.S. losses.

The performance of commanders and crews in this engagement is in the highest tradition of the United States Navy. But repeated acts of violence against the Armed Forces of the United States must be met not only with alert defense, but with positive reply. That reply is being given as I speak to you tonight. Air action is now in execution against gunboats and certain supporting facilities in North Viet-Nam which have been used in these hostile operations.

In the larger sense this new act of aggression, aimed directly at our own forces, again brings home to all of us in the United States the importance of the struggle for peace and security in southeast Asia. Aggression by terror against the peaceful villagers of South Viet-Nam has now been joined by open aggression on the high seas against the United States of America.

The determination of all Americans to carry out our full commitment to the people and to the government of South Viet-Nam will be redoubled by this outrage. Yet our response, for the present, will be limited and fitting. We Americans know, although others appear to forget, the risks of spreading conflict. We still seek no wider war.

I have instructed the Secretary of State to make this position totally clear to friends and to adversaries and, indeed, to all. I have instructed Ambassador Stevenson to raise this matter immediately and urgently before the Security Council of the United Nations. Finally, I have today met with the leaders of both parties in the Congress of the United States and I have informed them that I shall immediately request the Congress to pass a resolution making it clear that our Government is united in its determination to take all necessary measures in support of freedom and in defense of peace in southeast Asia.

I have been given encouraging assurance by these leaders of both parties that such a resolution will be promptly introduced, freely and expeditiously debated, and passed with overwhelming support. And just a few minutes ago I was able to reach Senator Goldwater and I am glad to say that he has expressed his support of the statement that I am making to you tonight.

It is a solemn responsibility to have to order even limited military action by forces whose overall strength is as vast and as awesome as those of the United States of America, but it is my considered conviction, shared throughout your Government, that firmness in the right is indispensable today for peace; that firmness will always be measured. Its mission is peace.

Appendix II

SENATE RESOLUTION 189

The entire text of S.J. 189 is in Cong. Rec. S18133 (Daily ed., August 5, 1964) and reads:

Whereas naval units of the Communist regime in Vietnam, in violation of the principles of the Charter of the United Nations and of international law, have deliberately and repeatedly attacked United States naval vessels lawfully present in international waters, and have thereby created a serious threat to international peace.

Whereas these attacks are part of a deliberate and systematic campaign of aggression that the Communist regime in North Vietnam has been waging against its neighbors and the nations joined with them in the collective defense of their freedom.

Whereas the United States is assisting the peoples of southeast Asia to protect their freedom and has no territorial, military or political ambitions in that area, but desires only that these peoples should be left in peace to work out their own destinies in their own way: Now, therefore, be it

Resolved by the Senate and House of Representatives of the United States of America in Congress assembled, That the Congress approves and supports the determination of the President, as Commander in Chief, to take all necessary measures to repel any armed attack against the forces of the United States and to prevent further aggression.

Sec. 2. The United States regards as vital to its national interest and to world peace the maintenance of international peace and security in southeast Asia. Consonant with the Constitution and the Charter of the United Nations and in accordance with its obligations under the Southeast Asia Collective Defense Treaty, the United States is, therefore, prepared, as the President determines, to take all necessary steps, including the use of armed force, to assist any member or protocol state of the Southeast Asia Collective Defense Treaty requesting assistance in defense of its freedom.

Sec. 3. This resolution shall expire when the President shall determine that the peace and security of the area is reasonably assured by international conditions created by action of the United Nations or otherwise, except that it may be terminated earlier by concurrent resolution of the Congress.

Appendix III

STATEMENT OF HONORABLE ROBERT S. McNAMARA, SECRETARY OF DEFENSE

Before Joint Committees of House and Senate Armed Services and Foreign Relations, August 6, 1964

Chairman Fulbright, Chairman Russell, and members of the Senate Foreign Relations and Armed Services Committees, during the past few days, deliberate and unprovoked military attacks by the North Vietnamese have given rise to the need for us to appear here today. I should like to review the attacks with you briefly and to describe the responses we made to those attacks.

The first incident occurred on August 2. It concerned the USS MADDOX, one of our destroyers engaged in *a routine patrol in International waters of the Gulf of Tonkin off the North Viet Nam coast.* At about noon, when the MADDOX was about 30 miles from the coast, she reported that three torpedo boats were on a southerly course heading toward the ship at a range of over 10 miles.

Two hours later, at approximately 2:40 P.M., the MADDOX was approached by a high speed—45 to 50 knots—craft. She reported that the apparent intention of the craft was to conduct a torpedo attack and that she intended to open fire in self-defense if necessary. She was attacked by the three PT craft at 3:08 P.M. She opened fire with her five-inch battery after three warning shots failed to slow down the attackers. The PTs continued their closing maneuvers, and two of the PTs closed to 5,000 yards, each firing one torpedo. The MADDOX changed course in an evasive move and the two torpedoes passed on the starboard side at a distance of 100 to 200 yards.

The USS TICONDEROGA, which was operating in waters to the southeast and which had been alerted to the impending attack, advised she was sending four already airborne F-8E (CRUSADER) fighters with rockets and 20 mm ammunition to provide air cover for the MADDOX. At about 3:21 P.M., the third hostile PT moved up the beam of the MAD-DOX and received a direct hit by a five-inch round; at the same time it dropped a torpedo into the water which was not sent to run. Machine gun fire from the PTs was directed at the MADDOX. However, there was no injury to personnel and no damage. The MADDOX continued in southerly direction to join with a sister destroyer, the C. TURNER JOY, as TICONDEROGA aircraft commenced attacking the PTs. XUNI rocket runs and 20 mm strafing attacks were directed against two of the PTs, and they were damaged. The third PT remained dead in the water and the aircraft escorted the MADDOX southward on its patrol course.

On Monday, August 3, the President made public instructions that he had issued the day before regarding future patrols and engagements with enemy craft. He instructed the Navy, first, to continue the patrols in the Gulf of Tonkin; second, to double the force by adding an additional destroyer to the one already on patrol; third, to provide a combat air patrol over the destroyers; and fourth, to issue instructions to the combat aircraft and to the destroyers (a) to attack any force which attacked them in international waters, and (b) to attack with the objective of not only driving off the force but of destroying it.

At the same time as these instructions were being broadcast throughout the world, the State Department, acting pursuant to the President's further instructions, took steps to deliver a note of protest to the North Vietnam regime. The note was also widely publicized. In concluded with the words, "The United States Government expects that the authorities of the regime in North Viet-Nam will be under no misapprehension as to the grave consequences which would inevitably result from any further unprovoked offensive military action against United States forces."

Our hopes that the firm defensive action taken in response to the first attack and the protest to Hanoi would end the matter were short-lived.

After the first attack on Sunday, the MADDOX joined with its sister destroyer, the USS TURNER JOY, in the Gulf of Tonkin and resumed its patrol in international waters, as directed by the President.

Monday, August 3, was uneventful.

The patrol was also uneventful during most of the daylight hours of Tuesday, August 4, however, the MADDOX reported radar contact with unidentified surface vessels who were paralleling its track and the track of the TURNER JOY. It was 7:40 P.M. when the MADDOX reported that, from actions being taken by those unidentified vessels, an attack by them appeared imminent. At this time the MADDOX was heading southeast near the center of the Gulf of Tonkin in International waters approximately 65 miles from the nearest land.

The MADDOX at 8:36 P.M. established new radar contact with two unidentified surface vessels and three unidentified aircraft. At this time, U.S. fighter aircraft were launched from the TICONDEROGA to rendezvous with the MADDOX and the TURNER JOY to provide protection against possible attack from the unidentified vessels and aircraft, in accordance with the President's previously issued directives. Shortly thereafter, the MADDOX reported that the unidentified aircraft had disappeared from its radar screen and that the TICONDEROGA arrived and commenced defensive patrol over the MADDOX and the TURNER JOY.

At 9:30 P.M., additional unidentified vessels were observed on the MADDOX radar, and these vessels began to close rapidly on the destroyer patrol at speeds in excess of 40 knots. The attacking craft continued to close rapidly from the west and south and the MADDOX reported that their intentions were evaluated as hostile. The destroyers reported at 9:52 P.M. that they were under continuous torpedo attack and were engaged in defensive counterfire.

Within the next hour, the destroyers relayed messages stating that they had avoided a number of torpedoes, that they had been under repeated attack, and that they had sunk two of the attacking craft. By Midnight local time, the destroyers reported that, even though many torpedoes had been fired at them, they had suffered no hits nor casualties and that the defensive aircraft from the TICONDEROGA were illuminating the area and attacking the enemy surface craft. Shortly thereafter, they reported that at least two enemy craft had been sunk although a low ceiling continued to hamper the aircraft operations. The TURNER JOY reported that during the engagement, in addition to the torpedo attack, she was fired upon by automatic weapons while being illuminated by searchlights.

Finally, after more than two hours under attack, the destroyers reported at 1:30 A.M. that the attacking craft had apparently broken off the engagement.

The deliberate and unprovoked nature of the attacks at locations that were indisputably in international waters compelled the President and his principal advisers to conclude that a prompt and firm military response was required. Accordingly, the President decided that air action, in reply to the unprovoked attacks, should be taken against gunboats and certain supporting facilities in North Vietnam which had been used in the hostile operations. On Tuesday evening, after consulting with Congressional leadership, he so informed the American people.

The United States military response was carefully planned and effectively carried out. The U.S. air strikes began approximately at noon Wednesday local time against North Vietnamese PT and gun boats, their bases and support facilities. These reprisal attacks, carried out by naval aircraft of the United States Seventh Fleet from the carriers TICONDEROGA and CONSTELLATION, were limited in scale—their primary targets being the weapons against which our patrolling destroyers had been forced to defend themselves twice in the prior 72 hours.

Specifically, our naval air forces launched 64 attack sorties against 4 North Vietnamese patrol boat bases and their boats and against a major supporting oil storage depot. Strike reports indicate that all targets were severely hit, in particular the petroleum installation where 10% of North Vietnam's petroleum storage capacity was 90% destroyed. Smoke was observed rising to 14,000 feet. Some 25 North Vietnamese patrol boats were destroyed or damaged.

Our losses were two aircraft destroyed and two damaged. One of the pilots is believed to have crashed with his plane between two PT craft he had under attack. Another pilot reported that he was ejecting from his downed aircraft. His whereabouts is at present listed as unknown.

In view of the unprovoked and deliberate attacks in international waters on our naval vessels and bearing in mind that the best way to deter escalation is to be prepared for it, the President and his principal advisers concluded that additional precautionary measures were required in Southeast Asia. Certain military deployments to the area are therefore now underway. These include:

  a. Transfer of an attack carrier group from the Pacific Coast to the Western Pacific;

  b. Movement of interceptor and fighter bomber aircraft into South Vietnam;

  c. Movement of fighter bomber aircraft into Thailand;

  d. Transfer of interceptor and fighter bomber squadrons from the United States to advance bases in the Pacific;

  e. Movement of an antisubmarine force into the South China Sea;

  f. The alerting and readying for movement of selected Army and Marine forces.

In the meantime, U.S. destroyers, with protective air cover as needed, continue their patrol in the international waters of the Gulf of Tonkin.

The moves we have taken to reinforce our forces in the Pacific are in my judgment sufficient for the time being. Other reinforcing steps can be taken very rapidly if the situation requires.

This concludes my descriptions of the two deliberate and unprovoked North Vietnamese attacks on U.S. naval vessels on the high seas; of the United States reprisal against the offending boats, their bases and related facilities; and of the precautionary deployment and alerting steps we have taken to guard against any eventuality.

Appendix IV

SECRETARY RUSK'S FULL STATEMENT

Chairman Fulbright, Chairman Russell, and members of the committees, I appear before you in support of the Joint Congressional Resolution on Southeast Asia now before your committees. If the committees are agreeable, I shall proceed by explaining the purpose of the Resolution. Secretary McNamara will then describe to you the recent attacks on our naval vessels and the U.S. response thereto. I would then propose to conclude by going over the text of the Resolution itself and discussing its meaning and scope.

The immediate occasion for the Resolution is of course the North Vietnamese attacks on our naval vessels, operating in international waters in the Gulf of Tonkin, on August 2nd and August 4th.

However, it is obvious that these attacks were not an isolated event but are related directly to the aggressive posture of North Vietnam and to the policy that the United States has been pursuing in assisting the free nations of Southeast Asia and particularly South Vietnam and Laos, to defend themselves against Communist aggression, and thus to preserve the peace of the area.

When Indochina was divided and the independent states of South Vietnam, Laos, and Cambodia were created under the conditions of the Geneva Accords of 1945, it was at once clear that in the face of the North Vietnamese threat South Vietnam and Laos could not maintain their independence without outside assistance. The government of South Vietnam turned to the United States for such assistance, and President Eisenhower in December 1954 made the decision that it should be furnished, stating that our purpose was to "assist the government of Vietnam in developing and maintaining a strong, viable state, capable of resisting attempted subversion or aggression through military means."

In the Fall of 1954, Secretary Dulles negotiated, and the Senate in early 1955 consented to, the Southeast Asia Collective Defense Treaty, sometimes known as the Manila Pact. This treaty provided for the collective defense of the parties to this treaty—Thailand, the Philippines, Australia, New Zealand, Pakistan, the United States, the United Kingdom, and France. It provided further that the protection of the treaty should extend, under an annexed protocol, to the territory of South Vietnam and to Laos and Cambodia.

I do not need to review for you the subsequent history of the North Vietnamese's efforts to subvert and conquer South Vietnam and to do the same in Laos. Having found that South Vietnam would not collapse of itself but was on the contrary making remarkable progress, Hanoi in 1954 initiated a systematic campaign of terror and subversion in South Vietnam, directed and supplied with key personnel and equipment from the North. By 1961, the situation had reached a critical point and the United States greatly increased its advisory and supporting assistance to the government of South Vietnam.

Despite this assistance, the task of countering the extensive Viet Cong effort remains a long and arduous one, and as you know we have moved within the last two weeks to further increase our support while recognizing always that the struggle in South Vietnam must essentially be the responsibility of the South Vietnamese themselves.

In Laos, the agreements reached at Geneva in 1962 have been consistently violated by Hanoi and in May of this year the situation took on a more critical character when a Communist military offensive drove neutralist forces from the area of the Plain of Jars they had held in 1962. Our responses to these events, including the provision of additional T-28's to the Government of Laos [deleted] are well known to you.

The present attacks, then, are no isolated event. They are part and parcel of a continuing Communist drive to conquer South Vietnam, control or conquer Laos, and thus weaken and eventually dominate and conquer other free nations of Southeast Asia. One does not need to spell out a "domino theory;" it is enough to recognize the true nature of the Communist doctrine of world revolution and the militant support that Hanoi and Peiping are giving to that doctrine in Southeast Asia.

U.S. POLICY AND OBJECTIVES

Although the United States did not itself sign the Geneva Accords of 1954, Under Secretary Walter Bedell Smith made a formal statement that the United States "would view any renewal of the aggression in violation of the aforesaid agreements with grave concern and as seriously threatening international peace and security." We have repeatedly made clear that the independence and security provided for South Vietnam under those Accords was a satisfactory status for South Vietnam. All that is needed, as I have myself often said, is for Hanoi and Peiping to leave their neighbors alone.

The same is true with respect to the 1962 Accords for Laos. These provided a reasonable arrangement for the status of Laos, and what is needed, again, is simply that the Communist side should honor the commitments it undertook.

Above all, there can be no doubt of United States objectives for these nations and for the area as a whole. Here, as elsewhere, we believe that nations are entitled to remain free and to develop as they see fit. The United States has no military, territorial, or political ambitions for itself in Southeast Asia. We seek only the restoration of peace and the removal of Communist subversion and aggression.

Essentially, the outcome of this conflict, and the course of events in the area as a whole, is up to the Communist side. It has the option of accepting the freedom and independence of neighboring nations, or of continuing its aggressive tactics. For our part, as President Johnson stated on June 23: "The United States intends no rashness, and seeks no wider war. But the United States is determined to use its strength to help those who are defending themselves against terror and aggression. We are a people of peace—but not of weakness or timidity."

PURPOSE OF THE RESOLUTION

This, then, is the background of the Resolution before you. We have never doubted the support of the American people for the policies that have been followed through three administrations over a period of a decade. But in the face of the heightened aggression on the Communist side, exemplified by these latest North Vietnamese attacks, it has seemed clearly wise to seek in the most emphatic form a declaration of Congressional support both for the defense of our armed forces against similar attacks and for the carrying forward of whatever steps may become necessary to assist the free nations covered by the Southeast Asia Treaty.

We cannot tell what steps may in the future be required to meet Communist aggression in Southeast Asia. The unity and determination of the American people, through their Congress, should be declared in terms so firm that they cannot possibly be mistaken by other nations. The world has learned over 50 years of history that aggression is invited if there is doubt about the response. Let us leave today's aggressors in no doubt whatever.

I now turn to Secretary McNamara, who will describe the recent attacks and our response.

I now turn to the specifics of the Resolution before you.

The preamble, I believe, speaks for itself. It spells out in the simplest and shortest terms possible the fact of North Vietnamese attacks, their relation to the over-all campaign of aggression by North Vietnam, and the purposes and objectives of the United States in Southeast Asia.

As to the operative sections of the Resolution, Section 1 declares the approval and support of the Congress for actions, in response to armed attack on United States forces, which the President has the authority and obligation to take in his capacity as Commander-in-Chief.

Turning next to Section 2 of the draft Resolution, let me make clear at the outset what the Resolution does not embrace. It does not cover action to assist any nation not a member of the Southeast Asia Treaty Organization or a protocol state. It does not cover any action in support of a nation unless such nation requests it. It does not cover any action to resist aggression that is not Communist in origin. The Southeast Asia Treaty includes a United States understanding that it is directed solely against "Communist aggression."

The language, "to take all necessary steps, including the use of armed force," is similar to the authority embraced in the Formosa Resolution of 1955, the Middle East Resolution of 1957, and the Cuba Resolution of 1962. Copies of each of these have been made available to you for comparative purposes. The Formosa Resolution authorized the President "to employ the armed forces of the United States". The Middle East Resolution stated that the United States was "prepared to use armed forces." The nearest parallel to the language of the present Resolution is in the first clause of the Cuba Resolution, that the United States is "determined . . . to prevent by whatever means may be necessary, including the use of arms" Cuban subversive activities extending to any part of the hemisphere.

I shall not take your time this morning to review the constitutional aspects of resolutions of this character. I believe it to be the generally accepted constitutional view that the President has the constitutional authority to take at least limited armed action in defense of American national interests; in at least 85 instances, Presidents of the United States have in fact taken such action. As I have said before, we cannot now be sure what actions may be required. The Formosa Resolution of 1955 was followed by the use of United States warships to escort supply convoys to the offshore islands in 1958; the Middle East Resolution was followed by President Eisenhower's sending of troops to Lebanon in 1958; the Cuba Resolution was followed by the well-known events of October 1962. I do not suggest that any of these actions may serve as a parallel for what may be required in Southeast Asia. There can be no doubt, however, that these previous resolutions form a solid legal precedent for the action now proposed. Such action is required to make the purposes of the United States clear and to protect our national interests.

Appendix V

WAS THERE A PRECEDENT FOR THE GULF OF TONKIN RESOLUTION?

In his message to Congress accompanying S.J. 189, President Johnson stressed that the resolution was similar to those passed in the Formosa Crisis of 1955, the Mid-East Crisis of 1957, and the Cuban missile crisis of 1962. This point was also made by Secretary Rusk in his statement at the August 6, 1964, hearing.

The language of each resolution was:

CUBA

Whereas President James Monroe, announcing the Monroe Doctrine in 1823, declared that the United States would consider any attempt on the part of European powers "to extend their system to any portion of this hemisphere as dangerous to our peace and safety"; and

Whereas in the Rio Treaty of 1947, the parties agreed that "an armed attack by any state against an American state shall be considered as an attack against all the American states, and consequently, each one of the said contracting parties undertakes to assist in meeting the attack in the exercise of the inherent right of individual or collective self-defense recognized by article 51 of the Charter of the United Nations"; and

Whereas the Foreign Ministers of the Organization of Ameri-

can States at Punta del Este in January 1962 declared: "The present Government of Cuba has identified itself with the principles
of Marxist-Leninist ideology, has established a political, economic, and social system based on that doctrine, and accepts
military assistance from extracontinental Communist powers, including even the threat of military intervention in America on
the part of the Soviet Union; and

Whereas the international Communist movement has increasingly extended into Cuba its political, economic, and military
sphere of influence: Now, therefore, be it *Resolved by the Senate
and House of Representatives of the United States of America in Congress assembled,* That the United States is determined—

  (a) to prevent by whatever means may be necessary, includ-
      ing the use of arms, the Marxist Leninist regime in Cuba
      from extending, by force or the threat of force, its aggres-
      sive or subversive activities to any part of this hemi-
      sphere;
  (b) to prevent in Cuba the creation or use of an externally
      supported military capability endangering the security of
      the United States; and
  (c) to work with the Organization of American States and
      with freedom-loving Cubans to support the aspirations of
      the Cuban people for self-determination.

FORMOSA

Whereas the primary purpose of the United States in its relations
with all other nations, is to develop and sustain a just and en-
during peace for all; and

Whereas certain territories in the west Pacific under the juris-
diction of the Republic of China are now under armed attack,
and threats and declarations have been and are being made by
the Chinese Communists that such armed attacks in aid of and
in preparation for armed attack on Formosa and the Pescadores,

Whereas such armed attack if continued would gravely en-
danger the peace and security of the west Pacific area and particularly of Formosa and the Pescadores; and

Whereas the secure possession by friendly governments of the
western Pacific island chain, of which Formosa is a part, is essential to the vital interest of the United States and all friendly
nations in or bordering upon the Pacific Ocean; and

Whereas the President of the United States on January 6, 1955
submitted to the Senate for its advice and consent to ratification
a Mutual Defense Treaty between the United States and the Republic of China, which recognizes that an armed attack in the

west Pacific area directed against territories, therein described, in the region of Formosa and the Pescadores, would be dangerous to the peace and safety of the parties to the treaty; Therefore be it

Resolved by the Senate and House of Representatives of the United States of America in Congress assembled, That the President of the United States be and he hereby is authorized to employ the Armed Forces of the United States as he deems necessary for the specific purpose of securing and protecting the Formosa and the Pescadores against armed attack, this authority to include the territories of that area now in friendly hands and the taking of such other measures as he judges to be required or appropriate in assuring the defense of Formosa and the Pescadores.

This resolution shall expire when the President shall determine that the peace and security of the area is reasonably assured by international conditions created by action of the United Nations or otherwise and shall so report to the Congress.

MID-EAST

Resolved by the Senate and House of Representatives of the United States of America in Congress assembled, That the President be and hereby is authorized to cooperate with and assist any nation or group of nations in the general area of the Middle East desiring such assistance in the development of economic strength dedicated to the maintenance of national independence.

Section 2. The President is authorized to undertake in the general area of the Middle East, military assistance programs with any nation or group of nations of that area desiring such assistance. Furthermore, the United States regards as vital to the national interest and world peace and preservation of the independence and integrity of the nations of the Middle East. To this end, if the President determines the necessity thereof; the United States is prepared to use armed force to assist any nation or group of such nations requesting assistance against armed aggression from any country controlled by international communism: provided that such employment shall be consonant with the treaty obligations of the United States and with the Constitution of the United States.

This joint resolution shall expire when the President shall determine that the peace and security of the nations in the general area of Middle East are reasonably secured. . . .

The operative section of the Gulf of Tonkin resolution reads:

> Section 2. The United States regards as vital to its national in-
> terest and to world peace the maintenance of international peace
> and security in Southeast Asia. Consonant with the Constitution
> and the charter of the United Nations and in accordance with its
> obligations under the Southeast Asia Collective Defense Treaty,
> the United States is, therefore, prepared as the President deter-
> mines to take all necessary steps, including the use of armed
> force to assist any member or protocol state of the Southeast Asia
> Collective Defense Treaty requesting assistance in defense of its
> freedom.

The President is granted power to use armed force as he determines.
As Senator Nelson expressed it to me, "that opening was wide enough
to drive a truck through it." However the analogy to the Cuban resolution is false.

A careful analysis of the language shows that no unilateral power was
granted to the President to use force. The Cuban resolution is a declaration of policy (a) to prevent by whatever means may be necessary
including the use of arms the Marxist-Leninist regime in Cuba from extending by force, etc.

Nowhere is there a hint that "the use of arms" shall be determined by
the President unilaterally. It is difficult to assume that the vast difference
in language and the statements by Secretary Rusk and the President
drawing the analogy were erroneous. More believable is the likelihood
that an attempt was deliberately made to draw upon the prestige of
President Kennedy in support of language which was taken from President Eisenhower's resolutions. Whoever drafted the Cuban resolution
was surely aware of the language of the Formosa and Mid-East resolutions and deliberately drafted the language to avoid the unilateral grant
of the power of war to the President.

To maintain otherwise, as did Secretary Rusk and the President, must
be considered deliberate deceit. No other explanation fits.

Appendix VI

ADDRESS OF SENATOR JOHN F. KENNEDY, APRIL 6, 1954

MR. KENNEDY. Mr. President, the time has come for the American people to be told the blunt truth about Indochina.

I am reluctant to make any statements which may be misinterpreted as unappreciative of the gallant French struggle at Dien Bien Phu and elsewhere; or as partisan criticism of our Secretary of State just prior to his participation in the delicate deliberations in Geneva. Nor, as one who is not a member of those committees of the Congress which have been briefed—if not consulted—on this matter, do I wish to appear impetuous or an alarmist in my evaluation of the situation. But the speeches of President Eisenhower, Secretary Dulles, and others have left too much unsaid, in my opinion—and what has been left unsaid is the heart of the problem that should concern every citizen. For if the American people are, for the fourth time in this century, to travel the long and tortuous road of war—particularly a war which we now realize would threaten the survival of civilization—then I believe we have a right—a right which we should have hitherto exercised—to inquire in detail into the nature of the struggle in which we may become engaged, and the alternative to such struggle. Without such clarification the general support and success of our policy is endangered.

Inasmuch as Secretary Dulles has rejected, with finality, any suggestion of bargaining on Indochina in exchange for recognition of Red

China, those discussions in Geneva which concern that war may center around two basic alternatives:

The first is a negotiated peace, based either upon partition of the area between the forces of the Viet Minh and the French Union, possibly along the 16th parallel; or based upon a coalition government in which Ho Chi Minh is represented. Despite any wishful thinking to the contrary, it should be apparent that the popularity and prevalence of Ho Chi Minh and his following throughout Indochina would cause either partition or a coalition government to result in eventual domination by the Communists.

The second alternative is for the United States to persuade the French to continue their valiant and costly struggle; an alternative which, considering the current state of opinion in France, will be adopted only if the United States pledges increasing support. Secretary Dulles' statement that the "imposition in southeast Asia of the political system of Communist Russia and its Chinese Communist ally ... should be met by united action" indicates that it is our policy to give such support; that we will, as observed by the New York Times last Wednesday, "fight if necessary to keep southeast Asia out of their hands"; and that we hope to win the support of the free countries of Asia for united action against communism in Indochina, in spite of the fact that such nations have pursued since the war's inception a policy of cold neutrality.

I think it is important that the Senate and the American people demonstrate their endorsement of Mr. Dulles' objectives, despite our difficulty in ascertaining the full significance of its key phrases.

Certainly, I, for one, favor a policy of a "united action" by many nations whenever necessary to achieve a military and political victory for the free world in that area, realizing full well that it may eventually require some commitment of our manpower.

But to pour money, material, and men into the jungles of Indochina without at least a remote prospect of victory would be dangerously futile and self destructive. Of course, all discussion of "united action" assumes the inevitability of such victory; but such assumptions are not unlike similar predictions of confidence which have lulled the American people for many years and which, if continued, would present an improper basis for determining the extent of American participation.

Permit me to review briefly some of the statements concerning the progress of the war in that area, and it will be understood why I say that either we have not frankly and fully faced the seriousness of the military situation, or our intelligence estimates and those of the French have been woefully defective.

In February of 1951, for example, the late Brig. Gen. Francis G. Brink, then head of the United States Military Advisory Group, in Indochina, told us of the favorable turn of events in that area as a result of new tactics designed by General Jean de Lattre de Tassigny. In the fall of that same year, General de Lattre himself voiced optimism in his speech before the National Press Club here in Washington; and predicted victory, under certain conditions, in 18 months to 2 years, during his visit to France.

In June of 1952, American and French officials issued a joint communique in Washington expressing the two countries' joint determination to bring the battle to a successful end; and Secretary of State Acheson stated at his press conference that

*The military situation appears to be developing favorably. * * * Aggression has been checked and recent indications warrant the view that the tide is now moving in our favor. * * * We can anticipate continued favorable developments.*

In March 1953, the French officials again came to Washington, again issued statements predicting victory in Indochina, and again joined with the United States in a communique planning military action and United States support which would achieve their new goal of decisive military victory in 2 years.

In May of 1953, President Eisenhower and Secretary of State Dulles told the Congress that our mutual-security program for France and Indochina would help "reduce this Communist pressure to manageable proportions." In June an American military mission headed by General O'Daniel was sent to discuss with General Navarre in Indochina the manner in which United States aid "may best contribute to the advancement of the objective of defeating the Cummunist forces there"; and in the fall of last year General O'Daniel stated that he was "confident that the French-trained Vietnam Army when fully organized would prevail over the rebels."

In September of 1953, French and American officials again conferred, and, in announcing a new program of extensive American aid, again issued a joint communique restating the objective of "an early and victorious conclusion."

On December 2, 1953, Assistant Secretary of State for Far Eastern Affairs Walter S. Robertson told the Women's National Republican Club in New York—in words almost identical with those of Secretary of State Acheson 18 months earlier—that "In Indochina . . . we believe the tide now is turning." Later the same month Secretary of State Dulles stated that military set backs in the area had been exaggerated; and that he did not "believe that anything that has happened upsets appreciably the time table of General Navarre's plan," which anticipated decisive military results by about March 1955.

In February of this year, Defense Secretary Wilson said that a French victory was "both possible and probable" and that the war was going "fully as well as we expected it to at this stage. I see no reason to think Indochina would be another Korea." Also in February of this year, Under Secretary of State Smith stated that:

*The military situation in Indochina is favorable. * * * Contrary to some re-ports, the recent advances made by the Viet Minh are largely "real estate" operation. * * * Tactically, the French position is solid and the officers in the field seem confident of their ability to deal with the situation.*

Less than 2 weeks ago, Admiral Radford, Chairman of the Joint Chiefs of Staff, stated that "the French are going to win." And finally, in a press conference some days prior to his speech to the Overseas Press Club in New York, Secretary of State Dulles stated that he did not "expect that there is going to be a Communist victory in Indochina"; that "in terms of Communist domination of Indochina, I do not accept that as a prob-ability"; that "we have seen no reason to abandon the so-called Navarre plan," which meant decisive results only 1 year hence; and that the United States would provide whatever additional equipment was needed for victory over the Viet Minh; with the upper hand probably to be gained "by the end of the next fighting season."

Despite this series of optimistic reports about eventual victory, every Member of the Senate knows that such victory today appears to be des-perately remote, to say the least, despite tremendous amounts of eco-nomic and material aid from the United States, and despite a deplorable loss of French Union manpower. The call for either negotiations or ad-ditional participation by other nations underscores the remoteness of such a final victory today, regardless of the outcome at Dien Bien Phu. It is of course for these reasons that many French are reluctant to con-tinue the struggle without greater assistance; for to record the sapping effect which time and the enemy have had on their will and strength in that area is not to disparage their valor. If "united action" can achieve the necessary victory over the forces of communism, and thus preserve the security and freedom of all southeast Asia, then such united action is clearly called for. But if, on the other hand, the increase in our aid and the utilization of our troops would only result in further statements of confidence without ultimate victory over aggression, then now is the time when we must evaluate the conditions under which that pledge is made.

I am frankly of the belief that no amount of American military assis-tance in Indochina can conquer an enemy which is everywhere and at the same time nowhere, "an enemy of the people" which has the sym-pathy and covert support of the people. As succinctly stated by the re-port of the Judd Subcommittee of the House Foreign Affairs Committee in January of this year:

*Until political independence has been achieved, an effective fighting force from the associated states cannot be expected. * * * The apathy of the local population* *to the menace of Viet Minh communism disguised as nationalism is the most discouraging aspect of the situation. That can only be overcome through the grant of complete independence to each of the associated states. Only for such a cause as their own freedom will people make the heroic effort necessary to win this kind of struggle.*

This is an analysis which is shared, if in some instances grudgingly, by most American observers. Moreover, without political independence for the associated states, the other Asiatic nations have made it clear that they regard this as a war of colonialism; and the "united action" which is said to be so desperately needed for victory in that area is likely to end up as unilateral action by our own country. Such intervention, without participation by the armed forces of the other nations of Asia; without the support of the great masses of the peoples of the associated states, with increasing reluctance and discouragement on the part of the French—and, I might add, with hordes of Chinese Communist troops poised just across the border in anticipation of our unilateral entry into their kind of battleground—such intervention, Mr. President, would be virtually impossible in the type of military situation which prevails in Indochina.

This is not a new point, of course. In November of 1951, I reported upon my return from the Far East as follows:

In Indochina we have allied ourselves to the desperate effort of a French regime to hang on to the remnants of empire. There is no broad, general support of the native Vietnam Government among the people of that area. To check the southern drive of communism makes sense but not only through reliance on the force of arms. The task is rather to build strong native non-Communist sentiment within these areas and rely on that as a spearhead of defense rather than upon the legions of General de Lattre. To do this apart from and in defiance of innately nationalistic aims spells foredoomed failure.

In June of last year, I sought an amendment to the Mutual Security Act which would have provided for the distribution of American aid, to the extent feasible, in such a way as to encourage the freedom and independence desired by the people of the Associated States. My amendment was soundly defeated on the grounds that we should not pressure France into taking action on this delicate situation, and the new French Government could be expected to make "a decision which would obviate the necessity of this kind of amendment or resolution." The distinguished majority leader [Mr. Knowland] assured us that "We will all work, in conjunction with our great ally, France, toward the freedom of the people of those states."

It is true that only two days later on July 3 the French Government issued a statement agreeing that

There is every reason to complete the independence of sovereignty of the Associated States of Indochina by insuring * * * the transfer of the powers * * *

retained in the interests of the States themselves, because of the perilous circum-
stances resulting from the state of war.

In order to implement this agreement, Bao Dai arrive in Paris on August 27 calling for "complete independence for Vietnam."

I do not wish to worry the Senate with a long recital of the proceedings
of the negotiations, except to say that as of today they have brought no
important change in the treaty relationships between Vietnam and the
French Republic. Today the talks appear to be at an impasse; and the
return from Paris to Saigon of the Premier of Vietnam, Prince Buu Loc,
is not a happy augury for their success. Thus the degree of control which
the French retain in the area is approximately the same as I outlined last
year:

Politically, French control was and is extensive and paramount. There
is no popular assembly in Vietnam which represents the will of the people that can ratify the treaty relationship between Vietnam and the
French. Although the Associated States are said to be "independent
within the French Union," the French always have a permanent control
in the high council and in the Assembly of the Union, and the Government of France guides its actions. Under article 62 of the French Constitution, the French Government coordinates all of the resources of the
members of the Union placed in common to guarantee its defense under
policies directed and prepared by the French Government. French Union
subjects are given special legal exemptions, including the privilege of
extraterritoriality. The French High Commissioner continues to exercise
powers with respect to the internal security of the Associated States and
will have a similar mission even after the restoration of peace. When
Vietnamese taxes affect French Union subjects, there must be consultation with the representatives of the countries concerned before they are
imposed. The foreign policy of Vietnam must be coordinated with that
of France, and the French must give consent to the sending of diplomatic
missions to foreign countries. Inasmuch as the French did not develop
experienced governmental administrators before World War II, they
have guided to some degree actions within the local governments by
requiring the Vietnamese Government to turn to them for foreign coun-
selors and technicians.

Militarily, French control is nearly complete. The United States has in
the past dealt primarily with the French military authority, and these in
turn deal with the Associated States. Our equipment and aid is turned
over to the French who will then arrange for its distribution according
to their decision. The French are granted for a period of time without
limit facilities for bases and garrisons.

Culturally, the French are directly in contact with the training of intellectual youths of Vietnam, inasmuch as France joined in the establish-

ment of the university, installed a French rector, and provided that all instructions should be in French.

Economically, French control of the country's basic resources, transportation, trade, and economic life in general is extensive. In Vietnam, estimated French control is nearly 100 percent in the field of foreign commerce, international and coastal shipping, and rubber and other export products. The French control 66 percent of the rice export trade. Moreover, possession of property belonging to the French cannot be changed without permission of the French; and France shares the veto right under the PAU agreement on matters affecting France's export and import trade.

All of this flies in the face of repeated assurances to the American people by our own officials that complete independence has been or will be granted. In February of 1951, for example, the American minister to the Associated States, Donald Heath, told us that a French colonial regime had ended and that "all Indochinese Government services were turned over to the Indochinese States." This is untrue. In November of 1951, Assistant Secretary of State, Dean Rusk, again assured us that

The people of the Associated States are free to assume the extensive responsibility for their own affairs that has been accorded them by treaties with France.

Last year, the Department of States assured me that

France had granted such a full measure of control to the three states over their affairs that . . . these three countries became sovereign states.

In February of this year, Under Secretary of State Smith stated that the representatives of the government of Vietnam and of France would meet in Paris to draw up the treaty which will complete Vietnamese independence. As I have said those conversations began in July and broke off ten days ago. And again Secretary Dulles stated last week that

Their independence is not yet complete, but the French government last July declared its intention to complete that independence and negotiations to [sic] *that pledge are underway.*

They are underway nine months after the pledge was originally given.

I do not believe that the importance of the current breakdown of these negotiations has been made clear to the Senate or the people of the United States. Every year we are given three sets of assurances: First, that the independence of the Associated States is now complete; second, that the independence of the Associated States will soon be completed under steps "now" being undertaken; and third, that military victory for the French Union forces in Indochina is assured, or is just around the corner, or lies two years off. But the stringent limitations upon the status of the Associated States as sovereign states remain; and the fact that military victory has not yet been achieved is largely the result of these limitations. Repeated failure of these prophecies has, however, in no way diminished the frequency of their reiteration, and they have caused this Nation to delay definitive action until now the opportunity for any desirable solution may well be past.

It is time, therefore, for us to face the stark reality of the difficult situation before us without the false hopes which predictions of military victory and assurances of complete independence have given us in the past. The hard truth of the matter is, first, that without the wholehearted support of the peoples of the Associated States, without a reliable and crusading native army with a dependable officer corps, a military victory even with American support in that area is difficult, if not impossible, of achievement; and second, that the support of the people of that area cannot be obtained without a change in the contractual relationships which presently exist between the Associated States and the French Union.

Instead of approaching a solution of this problem, as Secretary Dulles indicated, French and Vietnamese officials appear to be receding from it. The Vietnamese, whose own representatives lack full popular support, because of a lack of popular assembly in that country, recognizing that French opinion favoring a military withdrawal would become overwhelming if all ties were entirely broken, have sought two treaties: one giving the Vietnamese complete and genuine independence, and the other maintaining a tie with the French Union on the basis of equality, as in the British Commonwealth. But nine months of negotiations have failed thus far to provide a formula for both independence and union which is acceptable to the parties currently in the government of each nation. The French Assembly on March 9—and I believe this action did not receive the attention it deserved—substantially lessened the chances of such a solution, through the adoption of a tremendously far-reaching rider which declared that France would consider her obligations toward Indochinese states ended if they should revoke the clauses in the French Constitution that bind them to the French Union. In other words, Mr. President, the French Parliament indicated that France would no longer have any obligations toward the Associated States if the present ties which bind them to the French Union—ties which assure, because of the constitutional arrangement of the French Union, that the French Republic and its Government are always the dominant power in the union—were broken.

I realize that Secretary Dulles cannot force the French to adopt any course of action to which they are opposed; nor am I unaware of the likelihood of a French military withdrawal from Indochina, once its political and economic stake in that area is gone. But we must realize that the difficulties in the military situation which would result from a French withdrawal would not be greatly different from the difficulties which would prevail after the intervention of American troops without the support of the Indochinese or the other nations of Asia. The situation might be compared to what the situation would have been in Korea, if the Japanese had maintained possession of Korea, if a Communist group of Koreans were carrying on a war there with Japan—which had dominated that area for more than a century—and if we then went to the assistance of the Japanese, and put down the revolution of the native Koreans, even though they were Communists, and even though in taking that action we could not have the support of the non-Communist elements of the country.

That is the type of situation, whether we like it or not, which is presented today in connection with our support of the French in Indochina, without the support of the native peoples of Indochina.

In Indochina, as in Korea, the battle against communism should be a battle, not for economic or political gain, but for the security of the free world, and for the values and institutions which are held dear in France and throughout the non-Communist world, as well as in the United States. It seems to me, therefore, that the dilemma which confronts us is not a hopeless one; that a victorious fight can be maintained by the French, with the support of this Nation and many other nations—and most important of all, the support of the Vietnamese and other peoples of the Associated States—once it is recognized that the defense of southeast Asia and the repelling of Communist aggression are the objectives of such a struggle, and not maintenance of political relationships founded upon ancient colonialism. In such a struggle, the United States and other nations may properly be called upon to play their fullest part.

If, however, this is not to be the nature of the war; if the French persist in their refusal to grant the legitimate independence and freedom desired by the peoples of the Associated States; and if those peoples and the other peoples of Asia remain aloof from the conflict, as they have in the past, then it is my hope that Secretary Dulles, before pledging our assistance at Geneva, will recognize the futility of channeling American men and machines into that hopeless internecine struggle.

The facts and alternatives before us are unpleasant, Mr. President. But in a nation such as ours, it is only through the fullest and frankest appreciation of such facts and alternatives that any foreign policy can be effectively maintained. In an era of supersonic attack and atomic retaliation, extended public debate and education are of no avail, once such policy must be implemented. The time to study, to doubt, to review, and revise is now, for upon our decisions now may well rest the peace and security of the world, and, indeed, the very continued existence of mankind. And if we cannot entrust this decision to the people then, as Thomas Jefferson once said:

If we think them not enlightened enough to exercise their control with a wholesome discretion, the remedy is not to take it from them but to inform their discretion by education.

Appendix VII

TEXT OF PRESIDENT JOHNSON'S SPEECH DELIVERED ON APRIL 7, 1965, AT THE JOHNS HOPKINS UNIVERSITY IN BALTIMORE

Mr. Garland, Senator Brewster, Senator Tydings, Members of the Congressional delegation, members of the faculty of Johns Hopkins, student body, my fellow Americans:

Last week 17 nations sent their views to some two dozen countries having an interest in Southeast Asia. We are joining those 17 countries and stating our American policy tonight which we believe will contribute toward peace in this area of the world.

I have come here to review once again with my own people the views of the American Government.

Tonight Americans and Asians are dying for a world where each people may choose its own path to change.

This is the principle for which our ancestors fought in the valleys of Pennsylvania. It is the principle for which our sons fight tonight in the jungles of Viet-Nam.

Viet-Nam is far away from this quiet campus. We have no territory there, nor do we seek any. The war is dirty and brutal and difficult. And some 400 young men, born into an America that is bursting with opportunity and promise, have ended their lives on Viet-Nam's steaming soil.

Why must we take this painful road?

Why must this Nation hazard its ease, and its interest, and its power for the sake of a people so far away?

We fight because we must fight if we are to live in a world where every country can shape its own destiny. And only in such a world will our own freedom be finally secure.

This kind of world will never be built by bombs or bullets. Yet the infirmities of man are such that force must often precede reason, and the waste of war, the works of peace.

We wish that this were not so. But we must deal with the world as it is, if it is ever to be as we wish.

THE NATURE OF THE CONFLICT

The world as it is in Asia is not a serene or peaceful place.

The first reality is that North Viet-Nam has attacked the independent nation of South Viet-Nam. Its object is total conquest.

Of course, some of the people of South Viet-Nam are participating in the attack on their own government. But trained men and supplies, orders and arms, flow in a constant stream from north to south.

This support is the heartbeat of the war.

And it is a war of unparalleled brutality. Simple farmers are the targets of assassination and kidnapping. Women and children are strangled in the night because their men are loyal to their government. And helpless villages are ravaged by sneak attacks. Large-scale raids are conducted on towns, and terror strikes in the heart of cities.

The confused nature of this conflict cannot mask the fact that it is the new face of an old enemy.

Over this war—and all Asia—is another reality: the deepening shadow of Communist China. The rulers in Hanoi are urged on by Peking. This is the regime which has destroyed freedom in Tibet, which has attacked India, and has been condemned by the United Nations for aggression in Korea. It is a nation which is helping the forces of violence in almost every continent. The contest in Viet-Nam is part of a wider pattern of aggressive purposes.

WHY ARE WE IN VIET-NAM?

Why are these realities our concern? Why are we in South Viet-Nam?

We are there because we have a promise to keep. Since 1954 every American President has offered support to the people of South Viet-Nam. We have helped to build, and we have helped to defend. Thus, over many years, we have made a national pledge to help South Viet-Nam defend its independence.

And I intend to keep that promise.

To dishonor that pledge, to abandon this small and brave nation to its enemies and to the terror that must follow, would be an unforgivable wrong.

We are also there to strengthen world order. Around the globe, from Berlin to Thailand, are people whose well-being rests, in part, on the belief that they can count on us if they are attacked. To leave Viet-Nam to its fate would shake the confidence of all these people in the value of an American commitment and in the value of America's word. The result would be increased unrest and instability, and even wider war.

We are also there because there are great stakes in the balance. Let no one think for a moment that retreat from Viet-Nam would bring an end to conflict. The battle would be renewed in one country and then another. The central lesson of our time is that the appetite of aggression is never satisfied. To withdraw from one battlefield means only to prepare for the next. We must say in Southeast Asia—as we did in Europe—in the words of the Bible: "Hitherto shalt thou come, but no further."

There are those who say that all our effort there will be futile—that China's power is such that it is bound to dominate all Southeast Asia. But there is no end to that argument until all of the nations of Asia are swallowed up.

There are those who wonder why we have a responsibility there. Well, we have it there for the same reason that we have a responsibility for the defense of Europe. World War II was fought in both Europe and Asia, and when it ended we found ourselves with continued responsibility for the defense of freedom.

OUR OBJECTIVE IN VIET-NAM

Our objective is the independence of South Viet-Nam, and its freedom from attack. We want nothing for ourselves—only that the people of South Viet-Nam be allowed to guide their own country in their own way.

We will do everything necessary to reach that objective. And we will do only what is absolutely necessary.

In recent months attacks on South Viet-Nam were stepped up. Thus, it became necessary for us to increase our response and to make attacks by air. This is not a change of purpose. It is a change in what we believe that purpose requires.

We do this in order to slow down aggression.

We do this to increase the confidence of the brave people of South Viet-Nam who have bravely borne this brutal battle for so many years with so many casualties.

And we do this to convince the leaders of North Viet-Nam—and all who seek to share their conquest—of a very simple fact:

We will not be defeated.

We will not grow tired.

We will not withdraw, either openly or under the cloak of a meaningless agreement.

We know that air attacks alone will not accomplish all of these purposes. But it is our best and prayerful judgment that they are a necessary part of the surest road to peace.

We hope that peace will come swiftly. But that is in the hands of others besides ourselves. And we must be prepared for a long continued conflict. Our resources are equal to any challenge. Because we fight for values and we fight for principles, rather than territory or colonies, our patience and our determination are unending.

Once this is clear, then it should also be clear that the only path for reasonable men is the path of peaceful settlement.

Such peace demands an independent South Viet-Nam—securely guaranteed and able to shape its own relationships to all others—free from outside interference—tied to no alliance—a military base for no other country.

These are the essentials of any final settlement.

We will never be second in the search for such a peaceful settlement in Viet-Nam.

There may be many ways to this kind of peace: in discussion or negotiation with the governments concerned; in large groups or in small ones; in the reaffirmation of old agreements or their strengthening with new ones.

We have stated this position over and over again, fifty times and more, to friend and foe alike. And we remain ready, with this purpose, for unconditional discussions.

And until that bright and necessary day of peace we will try to keep conflict from spreading. We have no desire to see thousands die in battle—Asians or Americans. We have no desire to devastate that which the people of North Viet-Nam have built with toil and sacrifice. We will use our power with restraint and with all the wisdom that we can command.

But we will use it.

This war, like most wars, is filled with terrible irony. For what do the people of North Viet-Nam want? They want what their neighbors also desire: food for their hunger; health for their bodies; a chance to learn; progress for their country; and an end to the bondage of material misery. And they would find all these things far more readily in peaceful association with others than in the endless course of battle.

A COOPERATIVE EFFORT FOR DEVELOPMENT

These countries of Southeast Asia are homes for millions of impoverished people. Each day these people rise at dawn and struggle through until the night to wrestle existence from the soil. They are often wracked by disease, plagued by hunger, and death comes at the early age of 40.

Stability and peace do not come easily in such a land. Neither independence nor human dignity will ever be won, though, by arms alone. It also requires the work of peace. The American people have helped generously in times past in these works. Now there must be a much more massive effort to improve the life of man in that conflict-torn corner of our world.

The first step is for the countries of Southeast Asia to associate themselves in a greatly expanded cooperative effort for development. We would hope that North Viet-Nam would take its place in the common effort just as soon as peaceful cooperation is possible.

The United Nations is already actively engaged in development in this area. As far back as 1961 I conferred with our authorities in Viet-Nam in connection with their work there. And I would hope tonight that the Secretary General of the United Nations could use the prestige of his great office, and his deep knowledge of Asia, to initiate, as soon as possible, with the countries of that area, a plan for cooperation in increased development.

For our part I will ask the Congress to join in a billion-dollar American investment in this effort as soon as it is underway.

And I would hope that all other industrialized countries, including the Soviet Union, will join this effort to replace despair with hope, and terror with progress.

The task is nothing less than to enrich the hopes and the existence of more than a hundred million people. And there is much to be done.

The vast Mekong River can provide food and water and power on a scale to dwarf even our own TVA.

The wonders of modern medicine can be spread through villages where thousands die every year from lack of care.

Schools can be established to train people in the skills that are needed to manage the process of development.

And these objectives, and more, are within the reach of a cooperative and determined effort.

I also intend to expand and speed up a program to make available our farm surpluses to assist in feeding and clothing the needy in Asia. We should not allow people to go hungry and wear rags while our own warehouses overflow with an abundance of wheat, corn, rice, and cotton.

So I will very shortly name a special team of outstanding, patriotic, distinguished Americans to inaugurate our participation in these programs. This team will be headed by Mr. Eugene Black, the very able former President of the World Bank.

In areas that are still ripped by conflict, of course development will not be easy. Peace will be necessary for final success. But we cannot and must not wait for peace to begin this job.

THE DREAM OF WORLD ORDER

This will be a disorderly planet for a long time. In Asia, as elsewhere, the forces of the modern world are shaking old ways and uprooting ancient civilizations. There will be turbulence and struggle and even violence. Great social change—as we see in our own country now—does not always come without conflict.

We must also expect that nations will on occasion be in dispute with us. It may be because we are rich, or powerful, or because we have made some mistakes, or because they honestly fear our intentions. However, no nation need ever fear that we desire their land, or to impose our will, or to dictate their institutions.

But we will always oppose the effort of one nation to conquer another nation.

We will do this because our own security is at stake.

But there is more to it than that. For our generation has a dream. It is a very old dream. But we have the power and now we have the opportunity to make that dream come true.

For centuries nations have struggled among each other. But we dream of a world where disputes are settled by law and reason. And we will try to make it so.

For most of history men have hated and killed one another in battle. But we dream of an end to war. And we will try to make it so.

For all existence most have lived in poverty, threatened by hunger. But we dream of a world where all are fed and charged with hope. And we will help to make it so.

The ordinary men and women of North Viet-Nam and South Viet-Nam—of China and India—of Russia and America—are brave people. They are filled with the same proportions of hate and fear, of love and hope. Most of them want the same things for themselves and their families. Most of them do not want their sons to ever die in battle, or see their homes, or the homes of others destroyed.

Well, this can be their world yet. Man now has the knowledge—always before denied—to make this planet serve the real needs of the people who live on it.

I know this will not be easy. I know how difficult it is for reason to guide passion, and love to master hate. The complexities of this world do not bow easily to pure and consistent answers.

But the simple truths are there just the same. We must all try to follow them as best we can.

CONCLUSION

We often say how impressive power is. But I do not find it impressive at all. The guns and the bombs, the rockets and the warships, are all symbols of human failure. They are necessary symbols. They protect what we cherish. But they are witness to human folly.

A dam built across a great river is impressive.

In the countryside where I was born, and where I live, I have seen the night illuminated, and the kitchens warmed, and the homes heated, where once the cheerless night and the ceaseless cold held sway. And all this happened because electricity came to our area along the humming wires of the REA. Electrification of the countryside—yes, that, too, is impressive.

A rich harvest in a hungry land is impressive.

These—not mighty arms—are the achievements which the American Nation believes to be impressive.

And, if we are steadfast, the time may come when all other nations will also find it so.

Every night before I turn out the lights to sleep I ask myself this question: Have I done everything that I can do to unite this country? Have I done everything I can to help unite the world, to try to bring peace and hope to all the peoples of the world? Have I done enough?

Ask yourselves that question in your homes—and in this hall tonight. Have we, each of us, all done all we could? Have we done enough?

We may well be living in the time foretold many years ago when it was said: "I call heaven and earth to record this day against you, that I have set before you life and death, blessing and cursing: therefore choose life, that both thou and thy seed may live."

This generation of the world must choose: destroy or build, kill or aid, hate or understand.

We can do all these things on a scale never dreamed of before.

We, we will choose life. In so doing we will prevail over the enemies within man, and over the natural enemies of all mankind.

To Dr. Eisenhower and Mr. Garland, and this great institution, Johns Hopkins, I thank you for this opportunity to convey my thoughts to you and to the American people.

Good night.

Appendix VIII

TEXT OF PRESIDENTIAL MESSAGE ACCOMPANYING H.J. RESOLUTION 447

A Supplemental Military Appropriation Bill for $700 Million, from Cong. Rec. S9492–3 (Daily ed., May 5, 1965)

To the Congress of the United States:

I ask the congress to appropriate at the earliest possible moment an additional 700 million dollars to meet mounting military requirements in Viet-Nam.

This is not a routine appropriation, for each member of Congress who supports this request is also voting to persist in our effort to halt communist aggression in South Viet-Nam. Each is saying that the Congress and the President stand united before the world in joint determination that the independence of South Viet-Nam shall be preserved and communist attack will not succeed.

In fiscal year 1965 we will spend about 1.5 billion dollars to fulfill our commitments in Southeast Asia. However, the pace of our activity is steadily rising. In December 1961, we had 3,164 men in South Viet-Nam. By the end of last week the number of our armed forces there had increased to over 35,000. At the request of the Government of South Viet-Nam in March, we sent Marines to secure the key Danang/Phu Bai area; two days ago, we sent the 173rd Airborne Brigade to the important Bien Hoa/Vung Tau area. More than 400 Americans have given their lives in Viet-Nam.

In the past two years, our helicopter activity in South Viet-Nam has tripled—from 30,000 flying hours in the first quarter of 1953 to 90,000 flying hours in the first quarter of this year.

In February we flew 160 strike sorties inside South Viet-Nam. In March and April, we flew more than 3,200 sorties against military targets in hostile areas inside the country.

Just two days ago, we dispatched General C. L. Milburn, Jr., Deputy Surgeon General of the Army, to assist Unites States representatives in Viet-Nam in formulating an expanded program of medical assistance for the people of South Viet-Nam. We are contemplating the expansion of existing programs under which mobile medical teams travel throughout the countryside providing on-the-spot medical facilities, treatment, and training in rural areas.

The additional funds I am requesting are needed to continue to provide our forces with the best and most modern supplies and equipment. They are needed to keep an abundant inventory of ammunition and other expendables. They are needed to build facilities to house and protect our men and supplies.

The entire 700 million dollars is for this fiscal year.

The Secretary of Defense will today support this request before the appropriate Congressional committees.

Nor can I guarantee this will be the last request. If our need expands I will turn again to the Congress. For we will do whatever must be done to ensure the safety of South Viet-Nam from aggression. This is the firm and irrevocable commitment of our people and nation.

I have reviewed the situation in Viet-Nam many times with the Congress, the American people and the world. South Viet-Nam has been attacked by North Viet-Nam. It has asked our help. We our giving that help because our commitments, our principles and our national interest demand it.

This is not the same kind of aggression with which the world has been long familiar. Instead of the sweep of invading armies, there is the steady, deadly stream of men and supplies. Instead of open battle between major opposing forces, there is murder in the night, assassination and terror. Instead of dramatic confrontation and sharp division between nationals of different lands, some citizens of South Viet-Nam have been recruited in the effort to conquer their own country.

All of this shrouds battle in confusion. But this is the face of war in the 1960s. This is the "war of liberation." Kept from direct attack by American power, unable to win a free election in any country, those who seek to expand communism by force now use subversion and terror. In this effort, they often enlist nationals of the countries they wish to conquer. But it is not civil war. It is sustained by power and resources from without. The very object of this tactic is to create the appearance of an internal revolt and to mask aggression. In this way, they hope to avoid confrontation with American resolution.

But we will not be fooled or deceived, in Viet-Nam or any place in the world where we have a commitment. This kind of war is against the independence of nations. And we will meet it, as we have met other shifting dangers for more than a generation.

Our commitment to South Viet-Nam is nourished by a quarter century of history. It rests on solemn treaties, the demands of principle, and the necessities of American security.

A quarter century ago it became apparent that the United States stood between those who wished to conquer an entire continent and the people they sought to conquer.

It was our determined purpose to help protect the independence of the Asian peoples.

The consequence of our determination was a vast war which took the lives of hundreds of thousands of Americans. Surely this generation will not lightly yield to new aggressors what the last generation paid for in blood and towering sacrifice.

When the war was over, we supported the efforts of Asian peoples to win their freedom from colonial rule. In the Philippines, Korea, Indonesia and elsewhere, we were on the side of national independence for this was also consistent with our belief in the right of all people to shape their own destinies.

That principle soon received another test in the fire of war. And we fought in Korea, so that South Korea might remain free.

Now, in Viet-Nam, we pursue the same principle which has infused American action in the Far East for a quarter of a century.

There are those who ask why this responsibility should be ours. The answer is simple. There is no on else who can do the job. Our power is essential, in the final test, if the nations of Asia are to be secure from expanding communism. Thus, when India was attacked, it looked to us for help, and we gave it gladly. We believe that Asia should be directed by Asians. But that means that each Asian people must have the right to find its own way, not that one group or nation should overrun all others.

Make no mistake about it. The aim in Viet-Nam is not simply the conquest of the South, tragic as that would be. It is to show that American commitment is worthless. Once that is done, the gates are down and the road is open to expansion and endless conquest. That is why Communist China opposes discussions, even though some discussions are clearly in the interest of North Viet-Nam.

Moreover, we are directly committed to the defense of South Viet-Nam. In 1954 we signed the Southeast Asia Collective Defense Treaty. That treaty committed us to act to meet aggression against South Viet-Nam. The Unites States Senate ratified that treaty and that obligation by a vote of 82–1.

Less than a year ago the Congress, by an almost unanimous vote, said that the United States was ready to take all necessary steps to meet its obligations under that treaty.

That resolution of the Congress expressed support for the policies of the Administration to help the people of South Viet-Nam against attack—a policy established by two previous Presidents.

Thus we cannot, and will not, withdraw or be defeated. The stakes are too high, the commitment too deep, the lessons of history too plain.

At every turning point in the last thirty years, there have been those who opposed a firm stance against aggression. They have always been wrong. And when we heeded their cries, when we gave in, the consequence has been more bloodshed and wider war.

We will not repeat that mistake. Nor will we heed those who urge us to use our great power in a reckless or casual manner. We have no desire to expand the conflict. We will do what must be done. And we will only do what must be done.

For, in the long run, there can be no military solution to the problems of Viet-Nam. We must find the path to peaceful settlement. Time and time again we have worked to open that path. We are still ready to talk, without conditions, with any government. We will go anywhere, discuss any subject, listen to any point of view in the interest of a peaceful solution.

I also deeply regret the necessity of bombing North Viet-Nam.

But we began those bombings only when patience had been transformed from a virtue into a blunder—the mistaken judgment of the attackers. Time and time again, men, women, and children—American and Vietnamese—were bombed in their villages and homes while we did not reply.

There was the November 1 attack on the Bien Hoa airfield. There was the Christmas Eve bombing of the Brinks Hotel in Saigon. There was the February 7 attack on the Pleiku base. In these attacks 15 Americans were killed and 245 injured. And they are only a few examples of a steady campaign of terror and attack.

We then decided we could no longer stand by and see men and women murdered and crippled while the bases of the aggressors were immune from reply.

But we have no desire to destroy human life. Our attacks have all been aimed at strictly military depots for the infiltration of men and arms to the South. We patrol routes of communication to halt the invaders. We destroy ammunition dumps to prevent the use of the explosive against our men and our allies.

Who among us can feel confident that we should allow our soldiers to be killed, while the aggressor sits smiling and secure in his sanctuary, protected by a border which he has violated a thousand times? I do not believe that is the view of the American people or of the Congress.

However, the bombing is not an end in itself. Its purpose is to bring us closer to the day of peace. And whenever it will serve the interest of peace to do so, we will end it.

And let us also remember, when we began the bombings, there was little talk of negotiations. There were few world-wide cries for peace. Some who now speak loudly were quietly content to permit Americans and Vietnamese to die and suffer at the hands of terror without protest. Our firmness may well have already brought us closer to peace.

Our conclusions are plain. We will to surrender. We do not wish to enlarge the conflict. We desire peaceful settlement and talks. And the aggression continues.

Therefore I see no choice but to continue the course we are on, filled as it is with peril and uncertainty.

I believe the American people support that course. They have learned the great lesson of this generation: wherever we have stood firm aggression has been halted, peace restored and liberty maintained.

This was true in Iran, in Greece and Turkey, and in Korea.

It was true in the Formosa straits and in Lebanon.

Our people do not flinch from sacrifice or risk when the cause of freedom demands it. And they have the deep, abiding, true instinct of the American people: When our nation is challenged it must respond. When freedom is in danger we must stand up to that danger. When we are attacked we must fight.

I know the Congress shares these beliefs of the people they represent.

I do not ask complete approval for every phase and action of your government. I do ask for prompt support of our basic course: resistance to aggression, moderation in the use of power, and a constant search for peace. Nothing will do more to strengthen your country in the world than the proof of national unity which an overwhelming vote for this appropriation will clearly show. To deny and delay this means to deny and to delay the fullest support of the American people and the American Congress to those brave men who are risking their lives for freedom in Viet-Nam.

Appendix IX

LETTER OF APRIL 24, 1975, FROM FRANK VALEO TO SENATOR GAYLORD NELSON

At the time North Vietnamese troops were completing their victory and entering Saigon in 1975, the following exchange of letters and memos took place. Frank Valeo was secretary to the Democratic Senatorial Caucus, and in effect was Mike Mansfield's right hand. Following is his letter to Senator Nelson and his memo to Mansfield of several days earlier. The memo has not been previously published to my knowledge.

Francis R. Valeo
Secretary

United States Senate
Office of the Secretary
April 24, 1975

Dear Senator Nelson:

Here is a copy of my recollection of the conversation with the two Vietnamese Generals.

Frank

MEMO TO: Honorable Mike Mansfield
FROM: Francis R. Valeo
SUBJECT: Interview with two Vietnamese

At the request of Senator Nelson, I met with two former heads of State of the Government of South Vietnam. One was a General Kahn and the second was a General Ky. They were accompanied by a Rose Kushner who described herself as a free lance writer of Kensington, Maryland. In asking me to see the two generals, Senator Nelson said that he had come into contact with them by way of a neighbor and at whose request he had seen them. Senator Mansfield, he said, had to be on the Floor and suggested that the Vietnamese talk with me.

Kahn served as President in the period that General Maxwell Taylor was in Vietnam (1964 to early 1965). He had left office in a dispute with Taylor. Kahn had also resigned after a dispute with the American Ambassador, but he was in Saigon during Senator Mansfield's trip in 1965 and had talked with him. General Kahn carried most of the conversation.

The conversation disclosed that both had felt compelled to leave office in protest at the pressure from the American Ambassadors and military leaders to shift strategy toward military operations more heavily dependent on U.S. practices and heavy increases in direct United States military participation in the war.

Kahn said that he had recently been in contact with the Hanoi representative in Paris and also with the National Revolutionary Front of South Vietnam. He had also had exchanges with so-called Third Force representatives. From these contacts, it was clear to him, he said, that the front was prepared for a ceasefire. The rationale of their willingness to take something less than a full surrender, as had occurred in Cambodia, was their awareness that if the matter were pushed to the bitter end they would have sole authority and responsibility for reconstruction in South Vietnam. At that point, the United States and most of the rest of the non-communist nations would cut themselves off entirely from Saigon. At the same time, the problem of reconstruction in South Vietnam was beyond their capability and even with North Vietnamese aid, China, the Soviet Union and other communist nations, could only be counted on for limited assistance. There would be neither the rice or the other commodities that are essential to prevent massive suffering in the South. It will be at least several years before the country can be restored to the point that it will be able to take care of itself. In short, they seemed to be prepared for a compromise because they need a continuance of contact and assistance from outside in addition to Hanoi and other "fraternal" nations. At least for the short run, Kahn believes, the NRF means to seek a neutralist stance and a three-sided government in Saigon.

Kahn said that he was not interested in heading any replacement government for Thieu in Saigon. Nevertheless, Thieu had to be replaced as he saw it, if the compromise solution were to be possible. He said that the Third Force and non-communists such as himself, could move rapidly with the NRF to form a National Council in Saigon provided Thieu were removed and the United States were prepared to accept the substitute. He gave no indication how Thieu was to be removed, but left the strong impression that the only factor keeping him in power at this time was the United States Embassy in Saigon. If a compromise solution were to have any chance, the removal would have to happen in the next 10 days. As he saw it, it was not so much the activities of the communist military forces which were going to overwhelm Saigon, but rather that Saigon would collapse from within and the military defense would simply evaporate. If that happened then the prospect for a United Front would disappear in the collapse. He felt that the United States was being victimized by its own propaganda and misinformation if we believed that there were as many North Vietnamese divisions in the field in South Vietnam as had described in the press of late. The overwhelming factor was not North Vietnam, but the collapse of the Saigon military. That made it possible for a minimum number of North Vietnamese and NRF forces to achieve control of the country outside of Saigon. He said that in the event of a final assault on Saigon the great bulk of the heavy equipment would not be Vietnamese or Soviet, but rather United States tanks, howitzers, and even planes.

He reiterated that time was of the essence if there was to be any compromise and ceasefire in Saigon. Thieu could not only not hold the situation together, he could not even guarantee the safe evacuation of Americans and foreign nationals. He made it clear, in closing, his opposition as did Ky to any further U.S. military aid to Saigon and put the stress on humanitarian and related assistance.

SELECTED BIBLIOGRAPHY

BOOKS

Abel, Elie. *The Missile Crisis*. Bantam ed. London: MacGibbon and Kee, 1966.

Aiken, George D. *Aiken Senate Diary, January 1972: January 1975*. Brattleboro, Vt.: Stephen Greene Press, 1976.

Ashby, LeRoy, and Rod Cramer. *Fighting the Odds*. Pullman: Washington State University Press, 1994.

Austin, Anthony. *The President's War*. New York: J. B. Lippincott, 1971.

Ball, George. *The Past Has Another Pattern*. New York: W. W. Norton, 1982.

Barrett, David M. *Uncertain Warriors*. Lawrence: University of Kansas Press, 1993.

Beschloss, Michael. *Taking Charge: The Johnson White House Tapes, 1963–64*. New York: Simon and Schuster, 1997.

Churchill, Winston. *In Memoriam*. New York: Bantam Books, 1965.

Effros, William G. *Quotations Vietnam, 1945–1970*. New York: Random House, 1970.

Eisenhower, Dwight D. *Public Papers of the Presidents of the United States: Dwight D. Eisenhower, 1953–61*, 8 vols. Washington, D.C.: Government Printing Office, 1960–61.

Fite, Gilbert C. *Richard B. Russell, Senator from Georgia*. Chapel Hill: University of North Carolina Press, 1991.

Gardner, Lloyd. *Pay Any Price*. Chicago: Ivan R. Dee Publishers, 1995.

Goodwin, Doris Kearns. *No Ordinary Time*. New York: Simon and Schuster, 1994.

Gruening, Ernest, and Herbert W. Beaser. *Vietnam Folly*. Washington, D.C.: National Press, 1968.

Halberstam, David. *The Best and the Brightest*. New York: Random House, 1969.

Hersh, Seymour T. *The Dark Side of Camelot*. New York: Little, Brown & Company, 1997.

Johnson, Lyndon B. *Public Papers of the Presidents of the United States: Lyndon B. Johnson, 1963–69*. 10 vols. Washington, D.C.: Government Printing Office, 1965–70.

Kaplan, Morton A., and Nicholas deB. Katzenbach. *The Political Foundation of International Law*. New York: Wiley, 1961.

Kennedy, John F. *Presidential Papers of the Presidents of the United States: John F. Kennedy, 1961–63*. 3 vols. Washington, D.C.: Government Printing Office, 1962–64.

Kennedy, Robert F. *Thirteen Days—A Memoir of the Cuban Missile Crisis*. Signet ed. New York: W. W. Norton, 1969.

McNamara, Robert. *In Retrospect*. New York: Random House, 1995.

Moise, Edward E. *Tonkin Gulf and the Escalation of the Vietnam War*. Chapel Hill: University of North Carolina Press, 1996.

Plaster, John L. *The Secret Wars of America's Commandos in Vietnam*. New York: Simon and Schuster, 1997.

Powell, Lee. *J. William Fulbright and America's Lost Crusade*. Little Rock, Ark.: Rose Publishing, 1984.

Powell, Lee R. *J. William Fulbright and His Time*. Memphis, Tenn.: Guild Bindery Press, 1996.

Prados, John. *The Hidden History of the Vietnam War*. Chicago: Ivan Dees Publishing, 1993.

Schandler, Herbert V. *The Unmaking of a President: Lyndon Johnson and Vietnam*. Princeton, N.J.: Princeton University Press, 1977.

Schlesinger, Arthur, Jr. *A Thousand Days*. Boston: Houghton Mifflin, 1964.

Schoenbrum, David. *Vietnam. How We Got In, How to Get Out*. New York: Atheneum, 1968.

Sorenson, Theodore C. *Kennedy*. New York: Bantam, 1966.

Stone, Isidore F. *In a Time of Torment*. New York: Random House, 1967.

United States Congress. *Biographical Directory of the United States Congress, 1774–1989: The Continental Congress, September 5, 1774, to October 21, 1788, and the Congress of the United States, from the First through the One Hundredth Congresses, March 4, 1789 to January 3, 1989*. Washington D.C.: Government Printing Office, 1989.

Wells, Tom. *The War Within: America's Battle over Vietnam*. Berkeley: University of California Press, 1994.

Windchy, Eugene. *Tonkin Gulf*. New York: Doubleday, 1971.

Wise, David. "Remember the Maddox." *Esquire*, April 1968, pp. 123–27.

Woods, Randall B. *Fulbright, A Biography*. Cambridge, England: Cambridge University Press, 1995.

Zhisui, Dr. Li. *The Private Life of Chairman Mao*. New York: Random House, 1994.

CONGRESSIONAL RECORD

Congressional Record. Daily ed. (28 July 1945): S8159.

Congressional Record. Daily ed. (28 June 1950): S9320–1.

Congressional Record. Daily ed. (6 April 1954): S4672.
Congressional Record. Daily ed. (17 February 1964): S2870.
Congressional Record. Daily ed. (17 February 1964): S2885.
Congressional Record. Daily ed. (31 March 1964): S6629–30.
Congressional Record. Daily ed. (23 June 1964): S14793.
Congressional Record. Daily ed. (23 June 1964): S14793–96.
Congressional Record. Daily ed. (5 August 1964): S18133.
Congressional Record. Daily ed. (5 August 1964): S18134.
Congressional Record. Daily ed. (6 August 1964): S18399.
Congressional Record. Daily ed. (6 August 1964): S18402.
Congressional Record. Daily ed. (6 August 1964): S18403.
Congressional Record. Daily ed. (6 August 1964): S18405–6.
Congressional Record. Daily ed. (6 August 1964): S18406–8.
Hearings on Southeast Asia Resolution, Congressional Record. Daily ed. (6 August 1964): S18409.
Congressional Record. Daily ed. (6 August 1964): S18415.
Congressional Record. Daily ed. (6 August 1964): S18416.
Congressional Record. Daily ed. (6 August 1964): S18417.
Congressional Record. Daily ed. (6 August 1964): S18420.
Congressional Record. Daily ed. (6 August 1964): S18425.
Congressional Record. Daily ed. (6 August 1964): S18459.
Congressional Record. Daily ed. (7 August 1964): S18444.
Congressional Record. Daily ed. (7 August 1964): S18446.
Congressional Record. Daily ed. (7 August 1964): S18459.
Congressional Record. Daily ed. (17 February 1965): S2886.
Congressional Record. Daily ed. (18 February 1965): S3188.
Congressional Record. Daily ed. (8 April 1965): S7493.
Congressional Record. Daily ed. (8 April 1965): S7494.
Congressional Record. Daily ed. (8 April 1965): S7496.
Congressional Record. Daily ed. (8 April 1965): S7497–98.
Congressional Record. Daily ed. (9 April 1965): S7665.
Congressional Record. Daily ed. (13 April 1965): S7805.
Congressional Record. Daily ed. (18 April 1965): S7498.
Congressional Record. Daily ed. (21 April 1965): S8125.
Congressional Record. Daily ed. (5 May 1965): S9500.
Congressional Record. Daily ed. (6 May 1965): S9729.
Congressional Record. Daily ed. (6 May 1965): S9752.
Congressional Record. Daily ed. (6 May 1965): S9754.
Congressional Record. Daily ed. (6 May 1965): S9759.
Congressional Record. Daily ed. (6 May 1965): S9772.
Congressional Record. Daily ed. (11 July 1966): S14496.
Congressional Record. Daily ed. (28 February 1967): S4720.
Hearings on U.S. Commitments to Foreign Powers (1967): S. 151.
Congressional Record. Daily ed. (24 June 1970): S21125.
Congressional Record. Daily ed. (24 June 1970): S21128–30.
Congressional Record. Daily ed. (24 June 1970): S21129.

INDEX

About the Author

EZRA Y. SIFF is a practicing attorney in Baltimore, Maryland. He was a legislative assistant to Senator Gaylord Nelson from late 1965 until 1968.